WORLD.WIDE.WEB

WORLD.WIDE.WEB
Chinese Migration in the 21st Century—
And How It Will Change the World

Bertil Lintner

Orchid Press

Bertil Lintner
WORLD.WIDE.WEB: Chinese Migration in the 21st Century—
And How It Will Change the World

First published in 2012 as *China Brothers* (in Korean), by Prunsoop
Publishing Co. Ltd., #529-3 Paju Book City, Munbal-li, Gyoha-eup,
Paju-si, Gyeonggi-do, Korea.

Copyright © Prunsoop Publishing Co. Ltd., Gyeonggi-do,
Korea, 2012.

First English edition, overall design and maps © Orchid Press,
Bangkok 2012.

ORCHID PRESS
P.O. Box 1046,
Silom Post Office,
Bangkok 10504, Thailand

www.orchidbooks.com

ISBN 978-974-524-150-3

CONTENTS

INTRODUCTION AND ACKNOWLEDGEMENTS

When the Mayflower dropped anchor inside the hooked tip of Cape Cod in November 1620, in what today is Massachusetts—and when the First Fleet sailed into Botany Bay in Australia in January 1788—the world would change forever. The Mayflower brought about a hundred English Separatists, better known in history as the Pilgrims, to the New World. In search of freedom of worship for their non-conformist kind of Christianity, they established a colony which they called Plymouth. It was not the first European settlement in North America—Jamestown in Virginia was established by the English in 1607 and the Dutch formed a colony in today's New York in 1614—but it brought a new kind of settlers to a vast continent, as they had no intention to return to their country of birth. It was an event that eventually led to massive migration and the birth of the United States of America, a predominantly Caucasian nation far away from Europe.

The eleven ships of the First Fleet carried 1,373 people, of whom 752 were convicts and convicts' children and the rest crew, marines and even a few ordinary passengers. They established the colony of New South Wales, thousands of miles from the English shore. At first, it was a penal colony but over time it attracted many voluntary settlers as well. On January 1, 1901, the Commonwealth of Australia was proclaimed, a self-governing part of the British Empire which then gradually achieved more independence.

Migration from Europe in the 19th and 20th centuries also led to the establishment of countries such as New Zealand, Canada, South Africa and, of course, the Spanish-speaking countries of South America, and Brazil with Portuguese as its official language. Other colonies were also established, even if those did not attract large numbers of settlers and were mainly sources of various kinds of raw materials that were needed in Europe during the industrial revolution. Nevertheless, European migration changed the map of the world and led to new balances of power that remain to this day.

Now, people from China are fanning out across the world, not to establish official colonies—that kind of migration is history—but in search of greener pastures, or freedom, or both. While exact figures are not available, Western intelligence officials believe that perhaps as many as two million people from the People's Republic of China, or PRC, have migrated legally or illegally since 1978. They estimate that 30,000-40,000 a year go to the United States—the preferred destination— and the same number to the rest of the world.

This is the third time in China's history that such a massive exodus has taken place. The first wave came after the fall of the Ming Dynasty in 1644 and consisted mainly of non-Mandarin speaking southerners who opposed the Manchu seizure of power in Beijing. These migrants established overseas Chinese communities all over Southeast Asia. The next wave came after the Taiping rebellion and other upheavals in the mid- and late-19th century as the Manchu Qing Dynasty crumbled and warlords and local chieftains tore the country into lawless fiefdoms. Not only did the migrants— again mainly from the southern coastal provinces—swell the existing Chinese communities in Southeast Asia, but newly invented steamships took them to North America, Australia and the Pacific.

This time, the migrants come from all over China. Better overland routes have led to a steady movement of people, primarily from the southern province of Yunnan, but also from Sichuan and Guangdong, to northern Thailand, Burma, Laos and Cambodia. Further afield, from the Russian Far east to the Pacific Islands, new Chinese migrants are making their presence felt. Entire families are also being smuggled to South Africa, where newly-established Chinese gangs operate under the guise of student organisations. Over the past two decades, even Japan and Korea, with their strict immigration laws and controls, have seen a massive influx of Chinese migrants. In Europe, thousands of Chinese have settled in Hungary—which now has a significant Asian population—and in France and the United Kingdom.

Contrary to popular beliefs, most of these migrants are not escaping from poverty or fleeing political prosecution. Many come from the richest parts of China, and pay fortunes to be smuggled to foreign countries. Few of them show any interest in politics in their new host countries. Rather, it is the dream of an even better life abroad that fuels the third wave of Chinese migration. While China is developing fast economically, expectations have also risen, and many seem to believe that those can best be fulfilled abroad.

With better communications and more information from the outside world reaching China, Chinese migration has been globalised, and it is already beginning to change traditional demographic patterns in places such as the Russian Far East and the Pacific region. And apart from the smaller groups of dissident students and intellectuals, the new migrants are not hostile to the Chinese government. On the contrary, as was shown in worldwide demonstrations by groups of overseas Chinese protesting the US accidental bombing of the Chinese embassy in Belgrade in May 1999, many remain patriotic and identify themselves with the "motherland."

A "World Wide Web" of Chinese communities is emerging, and it is a development that the authorities in Beijing view quite favourably, as Russian researcher Igor Saveliev of Japan's Niigata University has pointed out: "As a sending country, the PRC pursues policies of enhancing ties with overseas Chinese"—old as well as new migrants—to attract remittances and investment. At the same time, Saveliev states, "the PRC government's growing interest in migrants' activities overseas is frequently expressed in diplomatic missions' attempts to gather them in embassies and consulates by organising various events." Nyiri Pal, a Hungarian Sinologist who has had unique access to official Chinese records, has come to the conclusion that "increased migration from China and resurgent Chinese nationalism overseas is clearly linked to the PRC's great power aspirations."

China's official policy towards migration was expressed by the Shanghai New Migrants Research Project Team as early as 1995: "Since reform and opening, people who have left mainland China to reside abroad (called 'new migrants' for short) have continuously become more numerous. They are currently rising as an important force within overseas Chinese and ethnic Chinese communities. In the future, they will become a backbone of forces friendly to us in America and some other developed Western countries. Strengthening new migrant work has important realistic meaning and deep-going, far-reaching significance for promoting our country's modernising construction, implementing the unification of the motherland, expanding our country's influence and developing our country's relations with the countries of residence."

Judging from those documents, it is obvious that the Chinese authorities, while pledging to cooperate with the West, Japan and Korea to stem the flow of illegal migrants, are also viewing migration in a favourable light and, therefore, doing little or nothing to stem the flow of people leaving the country legally or illegally. There are three main reasons for this. First, it eases population pressure and alleviates unemployment in China. Migration serves as an important social safety valve in a country which, even before the current, global economic meltdown had a "floating" population of anywhere between 30 and 100 million people. In the wake of the global economic crisis, millions of more people have lost their jobs and may try to migrate to other countries, even if those are in a state of recession.

Secondly, remittances from overseas Chinese—old as well as new migrants—are a significant contribution to the Chinese economy. In Fujian province especially, entire towns and villages depend on remittances from abroad. According to William H. Myers, director of the Centre for the Study of Asian Enterprise Crime in Philadelphia and a former practising attorney specialising in immigration issues: "Between 1986 and 1994, migrant demand and the efficiency of the *shetou's* ("snakeheads" or people smugglers) services doubled the US Fujianese population twice, depleting the source of village population at the same rate. In some villages, like Hoyu in Changle County, 85 per cent of the inhabitants, including virtually all those of reproductive age, are in the United States. In others the average is 50 per cent, and none is without many families who have 'relatives' in the United States. Across all these counties 'women villages', whose populations consist primarily of single or married women and paternal grandparents who have not emigrated, have become commonplace." Not surprisingly, in many impoverished rural areas, such export of young, able men have contributed greatly to development in the shape of remittances from abroad.

And, thirdly, large Chinese communities abroad give the Chinese authorities friendly footholds in the countries where the migrants have settled. This reason is no doubt the most controversial, and could cause conflicts in some countries with a growing ethnic Chinese population. Hungarian sinologist Nyiri Pal wrote in May 2000: "Ideas of deliberate 'demographic expansion' by China as well as revived fifth-column theories—seeing overseas Chinese as a political pawn that can be mobilised by the Chinese government in international conflicts—are on the rise in various quarters: among politicians in the Russian Far East, journalists in Southeast Asia, and sometimes in the US media, as in the recent spying case of Chinese-American physicist Wen Ho Lee."

In the late 1990s, a string of revelations of Chinese industrial espionage in the United States had a severe impact on America's racial relations, and threatened to undermine the high level of acceptability that the Chinese-Americans have managed to achieve following decades of discrimination. Lee, a Taiwan-born scientist, worked for the University of California at the Los Alamos National Laboratory. A federal grand jury indicted him for stealing secrets about the U.S. nuclear arsenal for the People's Republic of China in December 1999. But investigators were unable to prove those initial accusations. In the end, the authorities were only able to charge Lee with improper handling of restricted data. In June 2006, he received 1.6 million US dollars from the federal government and five media organizations as part of a settlement of a civil suit he had filed against them for leaking his name to the press before any formal charges had been filed against him. The judge, James A. Parker, even had to apologize to Lee for the government misconduct of which he had been the victim.

But even if Lee was acquitted, the affair had some rather alarming consequences for public perceptions of Chinese migrants—and even Chinese residents who have been living for generations in the United States. Many became subjected to a new kind of blatant racism. Frank Ching, a Hong Kong-born Chinese-American wrote in the *Far Eastern Economic Review* in July 1999: "...virtually every Chinese is tarred—visitors, students, diplomats and business representatives. All are suspected of spying. Similarly, it is suggested that there are no legitimate Chinese companies—every one is considered to be a front for the Chinese military or some intelligence agency. It is assumed that every member of every Chinese delegation is on an intelligence mission, as is every Chinese student."

The anti-Asian hysteria had echoes of World War II, when every Japanese living in the United States was considered a spy, and nearly all of them were rounded up and interned in camps throughout the war. Thus, it is important to deal with this issue delicately so as not to foster racist sentiment. But even when treated factually and with caution, the reaction from some quarters can be hostile. When in April 2007 I wrote a three-part series about Chinese migration for *Asia Times Online*, it provoked a sharp response from ethnic Chinese readers. While some branded my series racist, a Malaysian calling himself "Truly Asian," went even further and wrote in a letter to the editor that it was "horribly unjust for one particular race to have grabbed North America, Australia and New Zealand...while the biggest losers are the overpopulated, then dying Asian empires like China and India. In fact, patriotic and nationalist Asians never quite accept this current status quo and lament at what a golden opportunity lost (and what a heavy price we paid) for our ancestors' folly for being weak at such a critical point in time in history. Take Australia and New Zealand, for example. We Asians are truly perplexed as to why and how two white 'potatoes' can be so ill-fitted into the midst of one giant Asian continent? Would it not be fairer, for the sake of world justice, for these two lumps of land to be proportionately distributed to overpopulated Asian countries like China, India, Indonesia, Japan etc.?...Perhaps it would be wise for White Australians to size-up and eventually sell out and ship back to North America and Europe before it is too late!"

Another, less aggressive letter writer asked whether Chinese immigrants are "any different from British immigrants or Israeli immigrants or even US immigrants?" But that was exactly my point. In the past, Europeans migrated to different corners of the world and today Chinese are doing the same. And, as European migration in the past changed the map of the world, Chinese migration to some areas may have an impact that could have far-reaching demographic and political consequences. I never said this was right or wrong, I was just observing what is happening. And this does not necessarily have to be a negative development. After the collapse of the Soviet Union in 1991, the United States emerged as the world's only, uncontested superpower. For better or for worse, the more recent rise of China as a global superpower has created some badly needed counterbalance to American dominance of the world. Many may argue that a bipolar world is better than one that is dominated by a single power. China, like the former Soviet Union, may not be a beacon of freedom and democracy. But, at least, the United States must take China's interests into consideration—as it had to consider Soviet interests during the Cold War—and that provides checks and balances that are in the interest of the world's smaller nations, which want to maintain their neutrality and independence of any superpower dominance.

On the other hand, stressing the importance of a bipolar world should not lead to acceptance of a new form of imperialism only because the "new superpower" happens to be an Asian country. This uncritical attitude has echoes of pre-World War Two sentiments among many Asian nationalists, who saw Japan as an ideal because it dared to challenge British, French, Dutch and American imperialism. Burmese nationalists, led by that country's independence hero Aung San, formed a group of 30 young men who underwent training in Japan—and returned to their country as the Burma Independence Army when Japan invaded it in January 1942.

With Japanese assistance, India's Subhas Chandra Bose organised the Indian National Army to fight the British. Indonesian nationalists like Sukarno and Mohammed Hatta openly stated that a Japanese advance on the then Dutch East Indies would be advantageous to their cause.

In the beginning, it was only countries which suffered from the onslaught of Japanese imperialism, such as Korea and China, that viewed Japan's rise in the region differently. In Burma, the nationalists discovered that the Imperial Japanese Army was even worse than the British in their treatment of the native population. In March 1945, Aung San and his comrades broke with their erstwhile Japanese benefactors and forged an alliance with the British. Three years later, Burma became an independent republic, free of any imperialist dominance.

Today's China is not behaving as aggressively as Japan did in the early and mid-20th century, but its influence is spreading—and it is important to remember that any superpower dominance, Asian or Western, over smaller nations poses a threat to national sovereignty. Chinese migration, like European migration in the past, is bound to lead to ethnic conflicts with the original inhabitants of the areas where the newcomers settle, and then not due to some imagined espionage activities but because land and businesses have been taken over by people who are considered outsiders. This has already happened in Papua New Guinea, the Solomon Islands and Tonga in the South Pacific and in some tribal areas in northern Burma.

While several Pacific nations have been rocked by violent anti-Chinese riots, bomb attacks were carried out against a Chinese hydroelectric power project in the Kachin area of northern Burma in April 2010. The power station was being built at the confluence of the Mali Hka and Nmai Hka rivers, a holy place for the Kachin people. The original inhabitants of the site for the dam—some 10,000 people—were forcibly evicted before the Chinese construction crews moved in.

Then, on September 30, 2011, Burma's new president, Thein Sein, stunned the world by announcing that the joint-venture mega-dam project had been suspended because "it was contrary to the will of the people." The US$3.6 billion dam would have been the world's 15th tallest and submerged

766 square kilometres of forestland, an area bigger than Singapore. And 90 per cent of the electricity was scheduled for export to China. Once online, it would have done grave harm to the Irrawaddy River, the nation's economic and cultural artery. A massive popular movement against the dam was gaining momentum and an escalation of anti-China tensions could have led to riots even more serious than in 1967, when angry mobs ransacked businesses and homes owned by ethnic Chinese in Rangoon, then the national capital. The future of Sino-Burmese relations—once close and cordial—is uncertain as Chinese plunder of northern Burma's natural resources and illegal Chinese migration into the country is upsetting local sentiments, a development that could also lead to potentially destabilizing splits inside the ruling military.

While investigating the impact of Chinese migration, I decided to focus on three parts of the world where Chinese migration may lead to demographic and perhaps even political changes: the Russian Far East, the South Pacific, and Burma, Laos and Cambodia in Southeast Asia. My travels took me to Vladivostok, Khabarovsk and Blagoveshchensk in the Russian Far East, New Zealand, Hawaii, Papua New Guinea, the Solomon Islands, Vanuatu, Fiji, Samoa, American Samoa, Tonga, the Marshall Islands, the Cook Islands, French Polynesia, New Caledonia, Guam and the Northern Mariana Islands in the Pacific. I also travelled locally in Southeast Asia, where I live, around northern Thailand and to Laos and Cambodia.

I was not able to visit Burma, because I remain blacklisted in that country for my critical reporting on its military government. But in Thailand I was able to meet and interview numerous people from Burma, and they provided me with insights into recent events in the north of their country. Over the years, I have also, on numerous occasions, visited Yunnan and other places in southern China as well as Japan, South Korea and Taiwan to collect information about passport rackets, people smuggling, and drug trafficking.

I am grateful to a number of people who directly or indirectly assisted me in writing this book. Many sources have to remain anonymous, especially those from China and Burma, who live in countries where sharing information with outside researchers can result in long prison terms, or worse. But among those I can name is my colleague Ko-lin Chin, the world's foremost expert on illegal Chinese migration and ethnic Chinese gangs in North America who also shares my interest in Burma and the Golden Triangle. My old friend Pan Ling, or Lynn Pan, has also written extensively about the Chinese diaspora from a national as well as overseas Chinese perspective. She was born in Shanghai and grew up in North Borneo, now the Malaysian state of Sabah.

It was not difficult to find people in Southeast Asia, the Russian Far East and the Pacific who were willing to talk about Chinese migration into their areas—and, especially in the Pacific, many expressed their anger at what they perceived as a massive influx of richer and more powerful outsiders. It was far more difficult to get Chinese migrants to talk openly about how they managed to reach their new host countries and settle there. Or to get Chinese officials to comment on illegal but often unofficially condoned migration to other countries. To cover those aspects of Chinese migration, I had to rely on the extensive research done by people such as Ko-lin Chin—a Burma-born Chinese who now is a prominent criminologist at Rutgers University in the United States. Other Sinologists were also helpful, and Nyiri Pal's translations of internal Chinese documents were invaluable for the understanding of unofficial attitudes to migration and its place in the broader context of China's national security—and its superpower ambitions.

In Russia my old friend Evgeniyi Belenky helped me interpret interviews and translate documents. In the South Pacific, Ben Bohane in Vanuatu and the late Robert Keith-Reid in Fiji were helpful and generous with information, as were Steve Marshall in Port Moresby, Papua New Guinea, and Ron Crocombe in the Cook Islands, the foremost expert on Pacific history and culture. Marie Noelle Patterson, the indefatigable crusader for better governance in her country, Vanuatu, first as Ombudsman and more recently as the local representative for Transparency International, taught me about the darker side of Asian as well as non-Asian investment in the Pacific region. Craig Skehan probably knows more about the Pacific than any other Australian journalist, and he put me on the right track in Papua New Guinea and other countries in the region. Anna Powles, a New Zealand academic, also provided valuable information about Chinese migration into her area of expertise, the Pacific islands.

I would also like to thank my friend Edward Loxton in Chiang Mai for proofreading the manuscript and tidying up my English. But, above all, I am grateful to the John D. and Catherine T. MacArthur Foundation for providing a research grant, which enabled me to take time off from my regular work as a journalist to travel to exciting countries and territories in the region to gather material for this book. I hope it will lead to a better understanding of migration patterns in the world today—and a sober acceptance of the fact that the map of the world may change again.

Chiang Mai, Thailand
December 2011

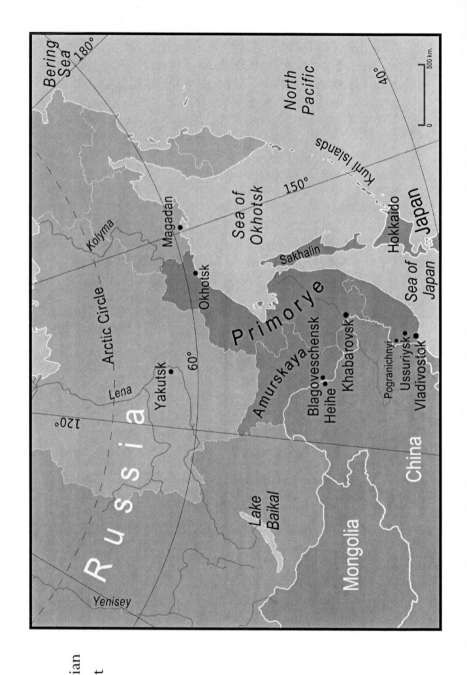

Map 1
The Russian
Far East

CHAPTER ONE
RULER OF THE EAST

It could have been one of the great Pacific Rim cities like Sydney, San Francisco and Vancouver. Nestled on the southern tip of a narrow peninsula, Vladivostok rises from the sea and spreads into the surrounding hills. It was founded during the time of the tsars and stately old buildings from that era still dominate the city centre. Architectural styles vary from classicism and baroque to Gothic and Art Nouveau. Vladivostok's central station—constructed in 1912 at the terminus of the Trans-Siberian Railway—has a similar design to Moscow's, 9,288 kilometres away. Other splendid buildings such as the Pushkin Theatre and the old Kunst and Albers department store make it a unique city on the edge of the Russian Far Eastern wilderness, and only 100 kilometres from the Chinese border.

But 70 years of communism has also made its mark. South of the Golden Horn Bay lies the First of May District, a grimy collection of Stalinesque, prefab apartment blocks. The streets are potholed and the suburbs, built during the Soviet era, are as dilapidated as the First of May District. Two thirds of Vladivostok's suburbs are so polluted that living in them is classified as a health hazard, according to Ecocentre, a local ecological organisation. Some areas are so polluted that they are defined as ecological disaster zones. The pollution comes from old Soviet-era, environmentally unfriendly industries such as shipbuilding and repairing, power stations, fur farming and mining.

Vladivostok is also the only Pacific Rim City that does not have an actual Chinatown. When Josef Stalin ruled the Soviet Union, most Asians in the Russian Far East were deported, the Chinese first back to China and then to labour camps, and ethnic Koreans to Uzbekistan, Kazakhstan and other Central Asian republics. From the mid 19th century to the Russian revolution in 1917, huge numbers of Chinese had actually worked in the Far East, clearing forests, mining for gold—and Chinese workers were employed to build parts of the Trans-Siberian Railway as well as Vladivostok's harbour. In 1896, gold was discovered in the Gilyui River basin in Amurskaya *oblast*, and thousands of Chinese went there and beyond to the gold fields of Yakutsk, but it was much more difficult to get to those remote parts of the Russian Far East.

In 1911 there were as many as 110,000 Chinese in the Far East and in 1917 they made up 30 per cent of the population of Vladivostok. They were businessmen and labourers and they worked in services and restaurants, bath houses and bakeries. In the centre of the city is an amazing labyrinth of narrow passageways with houses, yards and staircases. That is where the Chinese once lived.

The repatriation of the Chinese began shortly after the revolution. Many also left voluntarily as the new communist rulers nationalised industries and banned private businesses. The last batch of Chinese was deported in 1938, although some remained in remote settlements north and northwest of Vladivostok. But when relations between the Soviet Union and the new communist government in China began to deteriorate in the 1950s, most of the few remaining Chinese were rounded up, suspected of being spies and fifth-columnists. The Chinese accused the Soviets of being "revisionists", not true communists, and even "social imperialists."

But the tide is turning, and the Chinese are now coming back. Not in huge numbers and not yet permanently; many come for seasonal work and business with one foot in each country. It is true, however, that Chinese merchants now dominate the region's trade and commerce. Economically, the Russian Far East has already been separated from European Russia and integrated with China's. There are no reliable trade statistics from the area, but, as any visitor to the region can witness, Chinese business is everywhere and Chinese-made goods are abundant in all the markets. Chinese investment in hotels, casinos, real estate, and the construction sector is equally striking, as is the steady flow of scrap metal, timber and mineral resources leaving Russia by train and trucks for China.

Before the Soviet Union disintegrated in 1991, the Far East supplied European Russia and other western republics with fish and crabs from the Sea of Okhotsk. The area's heavy industry produced steel, aircraft and even ships, and few foreign consumer goods were for sale.

Today, Chinese consumer goods—which are cheaper and better than those produced far away in European Russia—and even food are flooding the markets, while timber and raw materials are going south, across the border to China. Entire factories are being dismantled and sold as scrap metal to China. And the seafood is almost exclusively sold to South Korea and Japan. Since the collapse of the Soviet Union, Chinese merchants have come across the border to sell clothes, tools, toys, watches and other consumer goods in a sprawling new market in one of Vladivostok's eastern suburbs. The newcomers from China are scattered in the suburbs or they are concentrated in other far eastern towns such as Ussuriysk and Blagoveshchensk, and in the smaller township of Pogranichnyi, where they now outnumber the European population.

Not all of them have entered Russia illegally. There is an acute shortage of labour in the Russian Far East, and at any one time there are 10,000-12,000 Chinese contract workers in the area, invited by Russian companies or working for Chinese-owned enterprises. Even according to the Russians I met in Vladivostok, they are preferred to local workers. A Russian academic expressed this in a paper on the Chinese in the labour market in the Far East: "They are highly organised and disciplined at work. As compared with local inhabitants, they do not drink and do not demand any immediate payments except some obligatory minimum." The Chinese are respected by many people in the Russian Far East because they work hard and take jobs that Russians are not prepared to do.

The problem of actual illegal migration—and the organised cross-border crime that inevitably has followed in its wake—is far greater and was deemed important enough to be highlighted in a joint declaration by Russia's then president Vladimir Putin and his Chinese counterpart Hu Jintao that was signed on May 27, 2003. Russia and China agreed to create a joint working group to curb the uncontrolled movement of people across the border. And facing racial prejudice and the threat of deportation, many choose—or are forced—to work for ethnic Chinese organised crime groups, the so-called Triads, which are spreading their influence over the Russian Far East. Organised crime gangs first became involved in the movement of people who needed assistance to circumvent the law and bribe local immigration officials and the police. Gradually, the relationship between many migrants and the gangs came to involve many other clandestine activities as well.

The rise in illegal migration and organised crime has fuelled racist attitudes towards all Chinese, even ordinary businessmen who are actually victimised by the Triads through their protection—or, more precisely, extortion—rackets. And the victims are usually fellow Chinese. According to a report by Viktor Larin, a Russian academic, extortion, robbery, murder and other criminal acts are committed both by Chinese and against Chinese, and account for two-thirds of all the crimes officially recorded in the Russian Far East.

At the same time, some argue that the prevailing perception that Chinese migrants are coming like a "tidal wave" is grossly exaggerated. In a paper presented at San Diego State University in California in January 2001, Russian academic Mikhail Alexeev emphasised that Chinese migration to the Russian Far East is not remotely similar to the Chinese presence in New York, San Francisco, or even Moscow.

In the long run, however, this development could nevertheless lead to demographic changes, when the floating population of Chinese traders and workers one day decide that they may want to stay. Russia's Far Eastern Federal District—a huge area covering 6,215,900 square kilometres—has only 6.7 million people. With slightly more than one person per square kilometre, it is one of the world's most sparsely populated areas. And the population has been rapidly declining since the collapse of the Soviet Union, as factories close down and military installations are withdrawn. In 1991, nine million people lived in the Far East, and the Russian government is now discussing a range of re-population programmes to avoid the forecast of 4-5 million people by 2015.

Across the border, China's three northeastern provinces—Heilongjiang, Jilin and Liaoning—are home to 100 million people, and the area has, even by Chinese standards, an unusually high unemployment rate, which has been rising even further since the worldwide economic meltdown of 2008. So the pressure is there and even if migrants from China do not exceed 200,000, or a mere 3 per cent of the total population—a figure often mentioned in the Russian press—many locals see it as a trend and believe that in another decade or two the numbers could be much higher. Anecdotal evidence also suggests that the official figure is far to low; most migrants do not register their presence with local authorities, and many move back and forth across the border making any kind of reliable "census" impossible.

Russia's Far East may be too poor—and the climate much too harsh with temperatures down to -40C in winter—to attract huge numbers of migrant workers. However, there is plenty of land, and thousands of Chinese farmers have settled in the border areas, where they grow vegetables and other crops. Local Russians told me their land was not suitable for farming, the weather being too cold most of the year. But the Chinese who have settled in the border areas have nevertheless managed to cultivate the land—and they sell the produce to local Russians. Officially, the Chinese cannot own land in Russia, but, according to Lyudmila Erokhina, a researcher at Vladivostok State University, Chinese businessmen have bribed local officials in order to acquire land from Russian farmers, and then they have brought in agricultural workers from China. A major problem is that Russia—despite the end of socialism—still has no law that regulates private ownership of land. As in the old days, all land belongs to the state, and individual farmers can only get the right to use it.

But more food—vegetables, fruit, pork, and even eggs—are brought in from China, which has led to concerns about food security in the Russian Far East. "The Chinese now dominate the agricultural sector and the food supply," Lyudmila told me when I visited her office in Vladivostok. "We're totally dependent on them." Findings during my own wanderings around markets in the Russian Far East support Lyudmila's fear. Not only electronic equipment and consumer goods but also items such as apples, strawberries and potatoes came from across the Chinese border. It was almost impossible to find any Russian-made provisions—apart from vodka, of which every supermarket had a generous supply.

Even more importantly, business opportunities abound, especially in the booming underground economy. Although it may be a trickle rather than a flood, Vitaly Nomokonov, director of the Centre for the Study of Organised Crime at the Far Eastern State University's Law Institute in Vladivostok, told me that the movement across the border is "unstoppable" and said that the authorities must make sure it does not damage what he called "Russia's national interests"—or, more precisely, to prevent foreign dominance of trade and commerce in the area.

Chinese gangs control many of the casinos in the region—there are more than a dozen gaming establishments around Vladivostok—as well as Chinese restaurants, and even some Russian hotels and eateries. The Far East has always been a stronghold for Russian crime groups, but many of their leaders have gone out of business or died in mysterious circumstances. Now, many small-time Russian gangsters work for Chinese syndicates, either as contacts for local business deals or as security guards at the casinos.

The most powerful crime lord in the Russian Far East is no longer a Russian godfather, but a Chinese man from across the border: Lao Da, "Elder Brother", who also goes under the names Li Dechuan and Liang Chuannan. His three gangs—The Wolves, The Snakes and The Mad Dogs—have effectively outmanoeuvred the old Russian godfathers and now control local gambling, tourism operations, and prostitution. They smuggle everything from fish—a very lucrative business in the Russian Far East—to illegal migrants, timber and narcotics, and regularly extort protection money from local Chinese as well as Russian businessmen. Nomokonov estimates that 15,00-17,000 tons of seafood worth 83 million US dollars is exported every year to Japan and South Korea, an estimated 70 per cent of it illegally. These are huge sums in Russia's impoverished Far East, and the profits are not deposited in Russian, but Japanese and South Korean banks—depriving local authorities of taxes and other revenue from the trade.

The once famous King Crab is becoming almost extinct as the fishing fleets scoop up whatever they can find in the Sea of Okhotsk Three million cubic metres of wood are smuggled to China annually from Khabarovsky *krai*. Even Siberian tigers, an endangered species, and mammoth ivory found in the region's wilderness are sold across the border.

Over the past few years, the networks of the Chinese underground banking system—which handles more money transactions in China and in overseas Chinese communities than are sent through official banks—have reached the Russian Far East to handle the new cross-border trade. In Chinese, the system is called *hui kuan*, "to remit sums of money" or *qiao hui*, "overseas remittances." Some refer to it as *fei qian*, "flying money." This informal banking system is swift, safe and free—and far more efficient than ordinary banks. And if the goods are illegal—payments could be for narcotics or other smuggled goods—then secrecy is of utmost importance. The system is built on trust, leaving no paper trail that could be scrutinised by international law enforcement agencies. In 2003 the daily turnover at the Chinese market in Irkutsk, which is called "Shanghai," was the equivalent of 300,000 US dollars, all in cash Russian or Chinese currencies, and transferred out through underground banks. Profits from Russian-run fishing fleets, on the other hand, are siphoned off to offshore bank accounts in Cyprus, and also never taxed by Russian authorities. This flow of black money, as well as lost income from the trade in seafood, is believed by crime experts to cost the government millions, perhaps billions, of rubles every year in lost revenue.

During my three visits to Vladivostok I was never able to assess the relationship between the local Russian criminals who remain in business and new Chinese crime bosses such as the notorious Lao Da. But it seems that the Chinese are far better organised and, therefore, have the upper hand. It was also difficult to determine how well-connected in high places he and his colleagues were. But enforcing the law—and curbing corruption within the police and local government—

has never been easy in this remote corner of Russia. In late 2002, the police actually arrested Lao Da and about a dozen of his associates, but the case collapsed and no one was brought to court. Typically, out of a total of 151 bribery cases filed in 2001 and 2002 in the Far East, only 20 made it to court—and, in the end, only one of the suspects received a prison sentence. In March 2007, Vladimir Nikolayev, the mayor of Vladivistok and a supporter of the ruling United Russia Party, was removed from office by a local court. He was convicted for abuse of power and received a suspended four and a half year sentence. The funds allegedly embezzled by Nikolayev totalled the equivalent of three million US dollars.

But such convictions are rare, and the central Russian authorities, far away in Moscow, are slowly losing both political and economic control over the Far East. On December 20, 2008, more than a thousand people protested against the imposition of higher import duties on non-Russian-made cars, a decision that came from Moscow. Most people in the Far East drive Japanese cars—even police cars I saw had the steering wheel on the right-hand side, as is the case in countries like Japan where they drive on the left-hand side of the road—and those vehicles are smuggled in from Niigata across the East Sea (which is also called the Sea of Japan), often with no duty paid at all. The local riot police were reluctant to suppress the rioters because they were sympathetic to the protests, which prompted the Russian authorities to airlift extra—and more loyal—police units from Moscow. They detained some protesters who were shouting "Putin, resign!" The protesters blocked roads and lit bonfires in the centre of Vladivostok, and for a brief period also blockaded the city's airport.

It is uncertain how the Chinese authorities view all these developments—including the spread of organised crime in the Russian Far East—but Lao Da seems to have no problem travelling back and forth across the border to visit his hometown of Shenyang in China's Liaoning province, where he is equally well-connected. This may be explained in the context of corruption, but it should also be remembered that Vladivostok and other cities in the Russian Far East were built on land conquered by the Russians from the Chinese in the 19th century.

Russian sovereignty over all territories north of the Amur River was recognised by the Chinese authorities under the treaties of Aigun and Tianjin in 1858, but with strong opposition from the Emperor at the time, Xianfeng of the Qing Dynasty. Given modern China's general attitude towards the "unequal treaties" of the 19th century, it is not far-fetched to assume that many Chinese consider large tracts of the Russian Far East lawfully theirs. A formal annexation of the Far East may not be possible, but as Chinese migration into the area continues—and Chinese businessmen of all stripes tighten their grip on the local economy—Moscow's ability to exercise effective control over its most remote federal district is bound to become even more tenuous.

The first Russian to establish a presence in Vladivostok was Count Nikolay Muravyov-Amursky, who founded a naval outpost there in 1859. He named it Vladikavkaz after a Russian fortress in the Caucasus and called it "the best of all ports." It soon became known as Vladivostok, "Ruler of the East," as more Russians settled there and the tsar wanted to show the rest of Asia who the new masters were. The Chinese, however, have always called it Haishenwai, literally "sea cucumber cliffs." It was not a proper town before the arrival of the Russians, but a French whaler who visited the Golden Horn—an inlet called so by its discoverers because it resembled Istanbul's Golden Horn—in 1852 found a fishing village populated by Chinese or Manchus on the shore of the bay, so they could claim that they were the original inhabitants of the area. Even other towns in the Russian Far East have Chinese names. Khabarovsk, the capital of the district, is called Pueli and Blagovechshensk Pushi is alternately Hailanpao.

But for decades, Vladivostok was a closed city even for ordinary Russians, who needed an "internal passport" to enter the area. There was no migration at all. Vladivostok was the headquarters of the Soviet Pacific Fleet and, as such, few outsiders were tolerated, But with the collapse of communist rule in 1991, effective control of Vladivostok first passed from the Navy to various gangs from other parts of the former Soviet Union. Gangsters from Azerbaijan, Armenia, Georgia, Chechnya and other Caucasian mountain regions moved in. The dreaded *yakuza*, Japan's organised crime groups, arrived from across the sea and set up shop, buying guns and whatever else they could scavenge from the ruins of the erstwhile superpower—and they brought in used cars from Japan. Then came the Chinese—ordinary law-abiding citizens as well as criminals—and they have managed to side-line all the other groups. And one can hardly blame the Chinese migrants for not abiding by Russian laws. According to Alexei Maslov, a Russian China specialist: "The arbitrary power of bureaucrats and the burden of federal and local taxes, no less then the plethora of permits and bribes needed to do anything, have made it almost impossible to run a business entirely legally even if one wanted to, and even if one could find law-abiding government officials with whom to cooperate."

In the early 1990s, people could just walk across the border to look for work in Russia, but in the late 1990s migration became more organised with "companies" arranging jobs and necessary documents, which almost invariably meant paying bribes to government officials. A main such organiser was Zui Je, deputy leader of a Chinese society in the Siberian town of Irkutsk and also local correspondent for the Chinese-language Moscow newspaper *Long Bao*, or "Dragon News." He arranged "invitations" for Chinese to stay in Irkutsk for a month or a year. He also helped the migrants obtain multiple-entry visas, international driving licences and other documents. Zui's society, Russians say, enjoys "special treatment" by the Chinese consulate in Irkutsk.

I first travelled to the Russian Far East in May 2003, and then again in April and July 2006. I found Vladivostok intriguing and even exciting. It was vibrant and full of energy—but it also reeked of crime and black money. The streets were not safe after dark because of the risk of being mugged by petty criminals. There were big godfathers, too, but not in the city's streets. Just north of Vladivostok, a road leads across the peninsula to a popular beach on the eastern side. The road is nick-named "the Black River"—and lined with palatial mansions surrounded by high walls. Only black money flows there, hence the name. Through the gates, I could glimpse well-manicured gardens with cypress trees, fountains and faux Greek and Roman statues. The contrast to other, squalid suburbs was striking, and I was told all the houses along "the Black River" had armed guards who would not hesitate to shoot on sight, if an intruder approached the property. This is the home of the kleptocrats who benefited from the transition from socialism to capitalism, and all of them are Russian. In recent years, ethnic Chinese godfathers may have become more powerful, but the Russian bosses are still involved in the illegal export of seafood to South Korea and Japan and timber and scrap metal to China. Foreign, not Russian, money has made them immensely wealthy. Given the importance of the cross-border trade with China, many of the Russian crime bosses now have mutually beneficial business arrangements with their Chinese counterparts.

There were not many Chinese in evidence in the streets of Vladivostok, although groups of visitors from the other side of the border could be seen in the hotels and the casinos. A Russian immigration officer I met told me that most Chinese workers—legal and illegal—in the Far East live in secluded communities and seldom venture out, perhaps out of fear of being victimized by xenophobic youth gangs, which are not as many and not as violent in the Far East as in, for instance, Moscow, but still exist.

Chinese workers live in dormitories, the officer told me, often inside factory compounds, where the only Russians are the guards. Agricultural workers also live on the farms, which are often surrounded by walls and fences. Until recently, most of them returned to China once their contracts are up. But that is changing, as Vilya Gelbras, a professor at Moscow State University and a China specialist, pointed out at a seminar in Blagoveshchensk in 2005: "Now every second Chinese arrives in Russia with a firm intention not to go back to China. Most of them cannot be classified as 'free migrants' anymore." Many acquire false documents, even citizenship, from corrupt local officials who are more than willing to accept bribes from Chinese and other foreigners than from their own people.

From Vladivostok, I travelled by train, 757 kilometres and an overnight journey along the Chinese border to Khabarovsk, a very different kind of town. Situated at the confluence of the Amur and Ussuri rivers far inland, it lacked the hustle and bustle of Vladivostok, a port city. But it has leafy boulevards, some lined with 19th century brick houses. One of the most popular restaurants in the town is Xianggang, where people after dinner danced to the tunes of cheesy ballads like Hotel California in front of the bar. There was even, just before midnight, an erotic show, not the kind of entertainment that is normally performed in eateries elsewhere. A scantily dressed Caucasian girl gyrated to the whining sound of Central Asian pipes in a Chinese-owned restaurant in the Russian Far East. In an odd way, it served as a reminder of the ethnic and cultural diversity of the erstwhile Soviet empire. And "Xianggang," of course, is "Hong Kong" in *pinyin*, the standard Romanisation across the border in the Chinese province of Heilongjiang.

The man who set up the restaurant, a Chinese from Heilongjiang, was murdered a few years ago, and it is now run by his widow, who uses a Russian name, Natasha. Xianggang is only one example of how Chinese influence is spreading beyond Vladivostok, and perhaps the most obvious because of its popularity among local residents. Everyone in Khabarovsk knows that Xianggang, and "Natasha's" success has become a symbol of the new assertiveness of Chinese-owned businesses in the capital city of Russia's Far Eastern Region.

But then, the vast forests north of Khabarovsk are also being cut down and the timber sent to China. And here, as elsewhere in the Russian Far East, people are leaving. The city was founded in 1858 as a military post and its first inhabitants were Russian and Ukrainian Cossacks, independent frontiersmen who staked out a life for themselves along the fringes of the Russian empires, often fighting the native Tartars.

The Russians had actually begun to expand their empire eastwards in the 17th century, into a vast wilderness then populated by nomadic and semi-nomadic tribes of reindeer herdsmen and hunters, distant relatives of the Lapps of northern Scandinavia and the Samoyeds of Russia's Arctic regions. Chinese chronicles from the Han Dynasty (206 BCE–220 CE) mention "fishskin tribes" (most probably the Nanai), "hairy people" (possibly Ainu, who survive in pockets of south Sakhalin, the Kuriles, and the northern Japanese island of Hokkaido) and a people called Yi-lou, whose curious habits included washing themselves in urine.

Inevitably, the Russians clashed with the Chinese, who claimed the same territories. Delegations from Moscow and the Manchu Court in Beijing finally met in Nerchinsk in August 1689. Following several weeks of negotiations, the two powers agreed on September 6th of that year that the frontier should run along the Argun, Shilka and Gorbitsa Rivers, and the crest of the "stone mountains" north and east of the Amur River. The Russians' expansion was halted, but they continued their conquest undeterred to the north and the east. Nothing could stop the Russians with their superior firepower, and then, in 1858, with a weak Emperor in Beijing, the Chinese finally had to concede defeat and withdraw to south of the Amur River.

Once the conquest had been completed, peasants from impoverished European Russia came, attracted by promises of free land. The tsars also deported all kinds of criminals to Siberia and the Far East. Between 1800 and 1914 at last one million people were exiled to the easternmost part of the Russian empire. As the demand for labour in the mineral-rich areas in the East increased, so did the list of punishable offenses elsewhere in Russia: vagrancy, prostitution, prize-fighting and even fortune-telling became grounds for banishment. The death penalty was abolished and replaced with exile and hard labour deliberately to encourage migration to the East. Russia's newly acquired territories had to be populated by Russians; the native tribes were pushed out and many perished from disease and hunger.

And, as was the case in America, fugitives of all kinds and members of non-conformist religious sects also migrated to this almost unchartered territory. It became Russia's "Wild East" where the Cossack represented the American pioneer, the Tartar the Red Indian and the Russian Army the US Cavalry. Khabarovsk got its name after an early Russian explorer—some would argue a Cossack—called Yerofey Khabarov. He had arrived there in the mid-17th century and was among those who then encountered Chinese forces. The new city was named in his honour when the area in the mid-

19th century came under effective Russian control and was opened for colonisation.

But that also meant that the European settlers in the Far East were exactly that, settlers and colonists. A local government official I met in Khabarovsk described the people of the Far East as "flowers without roots," adding that "all of us have an ancestral hometown or village in European Russia." Many of the new settlements in the Far East were named after towns and villages in European Russia, and even Russian "explorers," as the case of Khabarovsk. This government official and many others I met in the Russian Far East believed that 100 years from now, this region may no longer be part of Russia. The Chinese, on their part, would most likely view such a development as a natural consequence of their ascendancy as a regional power, and the ultimate goal of recovering all the lands that were lost to Western imperial powers in the 19th century.

China's economic dominance was even more evident in Blagovechshensk, a rather non-descript and not particularly attractive town of some 200,000 people further up the Amur River. The economy of Blagovechshensk is less developed and diversified than those of Khabarovsk and Vladivostok. Even the Trans-Siberian railway bypasses Blagovechshensk, and it is located at the end of a spur that branches off from the junction at Belogorsk. But it is on the banks of the Amur River where it forms the border with China—with the Chinese city of Heihe on the other side. Hydrofoils full of Chinese traders bringing in goods ply between the two cities every 30 minutes. There are some Russian merchants too—but they are also carrying household utensils, shoes and tools from China. European Russia is far away, and, incongruous as it may seem, these traders supply not only Blagovechshensk but the entire Amur region with consumer goods. And here, close to the border, ethnic Chinese traders are also much more in evidence in local markets than in, for instance, Khabarovsk and Vladivostok.

According to customs regulations, the duty-free baggage per person on these hydrofoils is limited to 50 kilogrammes. University students and unemployed youths are usually hired to go back and forth across the river, each time carrying just that, 50 kilogrammes of goods. According to a Russian report on the trade, the companies employing these "shuttle traders," as they are called locally, "are often owned by a Russian citizen *de jure* and by a Chinese citizen *de facto*." And if customs duties for some reason may be required, it can be settled in cash on the spot. The same Russian report stated, "Customs officers are most reluctant to be promoted to a higher rank because as soon as they are 'moved into an office,' no money of this kind will be available for them."

And it is not only the trade in consumer goods that is in the hands of the Chinese in Blagovechshensk. The town's construction sector is dominated by a Chinese-owned company, Hua Fu, which in 2006 began working on what will be the tallest building in the Russian Far East. The company is wholly Chinese owned and apart from two Russian welders, a crane operator and two guards, all the workers come from China. Chinese New Year is not an official holiday anywhere in Russia, but it is celebrated in style in Blagovechshensk with fireworks, drums and lion dances.

Even the mayor of the city and the governor of the area, Amursky *oblast*, usually participate as guests of honour. Amursky *oblast* may also be the most vulnerable for what many Russians, rightly or wrongly, call a "creeping invasion" by the Chinese. It is huge—363,700 square kilometres, the same area as Japan—but with a population of only 900,000. More than 35 million live in Heilongjiang across the Amur River.

In Blagovechshensk, Andrey Zabiyako, an academic at Amur State University, took me on a tour of the city. He is a descendant of Russian Cossacks; proud of his heritage and well versed in local history. Like Vladivostok, this city was also founded by Russians under the command of Count Nikolay Muravyov-Amursky, who conquered the area from the Manchurians. He decided to call it Blagovechshensk, which means "Good News."

But news may not be that good any longer. Andrey conceded that the gap between European and Asian Russia is widening. Russian culture is being marginalized, he said, and many people feel they do not have roots here. Many Chinese speak Russian, he told me, but few if any Russians speak Chinese. The Chinese are gaining the upper hand economically and even culturally, as they have the upper hand when it comes to languages—and therefore also when making business deals locally and across the frontier.

Andrey took me to a site on the Amur River, where a massacre of Chinese took place more than a hundred years ago—an event that few Chinese in the region are willing to forgive and to forget. In early 1900, a secret society called Yihequan, "the Fists of Righteousness and Harmony," began attacking foreigners and signs of foreign influence all over northern China. Dressed in brightly coloured clothing and wearing headbands with Chinese characters and religious amulets to protect them from "foreign bullets," their battle cry was *sha! sha!* ("kill"! "kill"!). Entire Christian families, including children, were hacked to death with swords. Churches and railway stations were burned, factories ransacked and telegraph lines cut. Then the rebels marched on Beijing. On June 13, 1901, they laid siege to the foreign legation quarter in the Chinese capital, which was defended by British, American, Russian, French, Italian and Japanese troops. The rebellion was crushed, but the seeds of extreme Chinese nationalism had been sown. The Fists of Righteousness and Harmony—or "the Boxers," as most foreigners called them—had shaken the foreign powers that dominated China at the time.

The Boxer rebellion spread as far north as Heihe, and even Blagovechshensk on the Russian side of the river, where many Chinese lived at the time. Some local Boxers fired handguns and hit the city jail. A rumour spread that they were going to use a cannon as well, which the local press somewhat irresponsibly reported, and anti-Chinese riots broke out in Blagovechshensk.

Many Chinese lived in an enclave called Trans-Zeya, a ten kilometre wide and 60 kilometre long enclave on the banks of the Amur. Cossacks and local Russian settlers attacked that area. Mobs robbed Chinese homes, and an order was issued for all Chinese—about 20,000 of them—to gather at one place to be deported. 6,000 showed up and were marched to the place by the Amur where Andrey had stopped his car. Soldiers and civilians pushed the Chinese into the river. There were no boats and few of the Chinese could swim. Shots were fired, and those who were not killed by bullets drowned in the river. Those who did not show up to be counted suffered the same fate a few days later. But not all Russians were xenophobic bigots, according to Andrey. Many Russian families hid their Chinese servants when the mobs ran amok.

The Chinese who remained in the Blagovechshensk area after the massacre were moved out in the 1930s, when the Japanese set up their puppet state in Manchukuo, and Stalin thought all Asians were potential fifth columnists for the Japanese. Unlike the Koreans who were relocated to Central Asia, the Chinese from Blagovechshensk perished in labour camps in Siberia, or were executed. Very few were left behind, and most of them were of mixed blood. Today Trans-Zeya is abandoned. No one wants to live there. The ghosts of the past may still be haunting the place, I am not sure, but a cold, eerie wind blew over the grassy banks of the Zeya River when Andrey showed me the place in May 2006.

After the split between China and the Soviet Union in the mid-1960s, China set up an academic group to collect information about the Blagovechshensk massacre. Some data and exhibits can still be seen at a museum in Heihe. And relations between China and the Soviet Union deteriorated even further during the Cultural Revolution in the late 1960s. The Chinese put up huge loudspeakers on their side of the Amur, which blasted anti-Soviet propaganda 24 hours a day into Russia. "I could hear it when I went to school in those days," Andrey told me as we were walking along the river. "The noise was deafening." In 1969, there was even a brief border war between China and the then-Soviet Union over some disputed islands in the Amur River near Khabarovsk.

But some Chinese actually fled to Russia during the Cultural Revolution, and some of them were recruited by the Soviet's intelligence agencies. The Russian author Yuri Ufimtsev, himself a former KGB station chief in Beijing, writes in his book *KGB v KHP: Skvoz Bambukovyi Zanaves*, or "KGB in China: A Peek Through the Bamboo Curtain," that 47 Chinese refugees arrived per month during the most violent days of the Cultural Revolution. The then-KGB chief Yuri Andropov, the longest serving and most influential chairman of the history of the agency, set up a "screening" unit in the Far East. An old prison was refurbished and turned into a holding centre, where Chinese refugees were debriefed. Those who were deemed to be "economic refugees" were repatriated to China, while those who were genuine political refugees were sent to *sovchozes,* state farms in the Khabarovsk area, where most remained while others were used for espionage work in China. Some were also sent to another camp near the Far Eastern coastal town of Magadan. The latter camp was established in 1970 and a Chinese settlement, which Ufimtsev calls "Little Chinatown," grew as a result. It is located at Elgen in the Kolyma area and it is still there.

The Chinese refugees who came in the late 1960s were given Soviet citizenship and they and their children are now Russian citizens. They are bilingual and are now being used by Chinese businessmen as fronts for their companies and activities, and to acquire property and get government documents. Old grievances are forgotten, and blood is no doubt stronger than politics.

Thus, the days of hostility across the Amur are over and the loudspeakers fell silent a long time ago. But today another message is being carried across the river. Even from the Russian side, it is easy to see that Heihe, with its new, modern buildings, is far more prosperous than Blagovechshensk. Trade and commerce, not old-style Maoist propaganda, now emanate from Heihe. The Russian Far East has become a backwater, a source of raw materials for the Chinese and a market for cheap consumer goods. Russia, once a superpower, now hobbles along in the shadow of the much wealthier and more powerful China.

So are China and the Chinese about to take over the Russian Far East? In Vladivostok, local Chinese have established the Vladivostok Union of Chinese and *Huaqiao* ("sojourners"), which has played its cards very cleverly as shown when, on May 2nd, 2002, a grand reception was organised to celebrate Russia's victory in the "Great Patriotic War"—which is what the Russians call World War II. That did a lot for image building, even if a local survey shows that 47 per cent of Russians in the Far East were sincerely convinced that there is a real possibility of the territory being annexed by China. And 28 per cent of respondents believed that the source of the threat was a "peaceful invasion by the Chinese." On the other hand, 43 per cent of Chinese in Vladivostok and 34 per cent in Khabarovsk thought that the attitude of local Russians to them was either bad or not very friendly. For that matter, they held the same opinion of Russian authorities, who were also seen as hostile, unhelpful and corrupt.

To improve bilateral relations and change attitudes on both sides, China opened a new consulate in Vladivostok in March 2005, in addition to the already existing consulate general in Khabarovsk. It was inaugurated with balloons and fireworks. Opening of the Vladivostok consulate will help Russia and China "reach their strategic goal of tripling trade by 2010," said Sergei Darkin, the governor of Primorye, a region that includes Vladivostok. Official trade at the time amounted to 829 million US dollars, and the figure would have been much higher if unofficial trade was included. Darkin should know; he was at the time also the director of a big fishing company. He is one of the biggest power brokers in the region and a millionaire.

Much of the real economic power in the Russian Far East now lies with the Chinese-Russian Industry and Commerce Union, which was founded in 2002. Its charter states that major goals are to "protect legal rights of its members through legal means, to facilitate Chinese businessmen who permanently reside in the Russian Far East and *huaqiao* in establishing contacts with Russian businessmen…and to participate in the development of the local economy and society." The actual Ruler of the East today may soon be China, not Moscow.

The movement may well be, as Vitaly Nomokonov at the Far Eastern State University's Law Institute says, "unstoppable." And one day Vladivostok may once again be known as Haishenwai. At least, that is what many Russians fear and, perhaps, what many Chinese would like to happen.

Map 2
The South Pacific

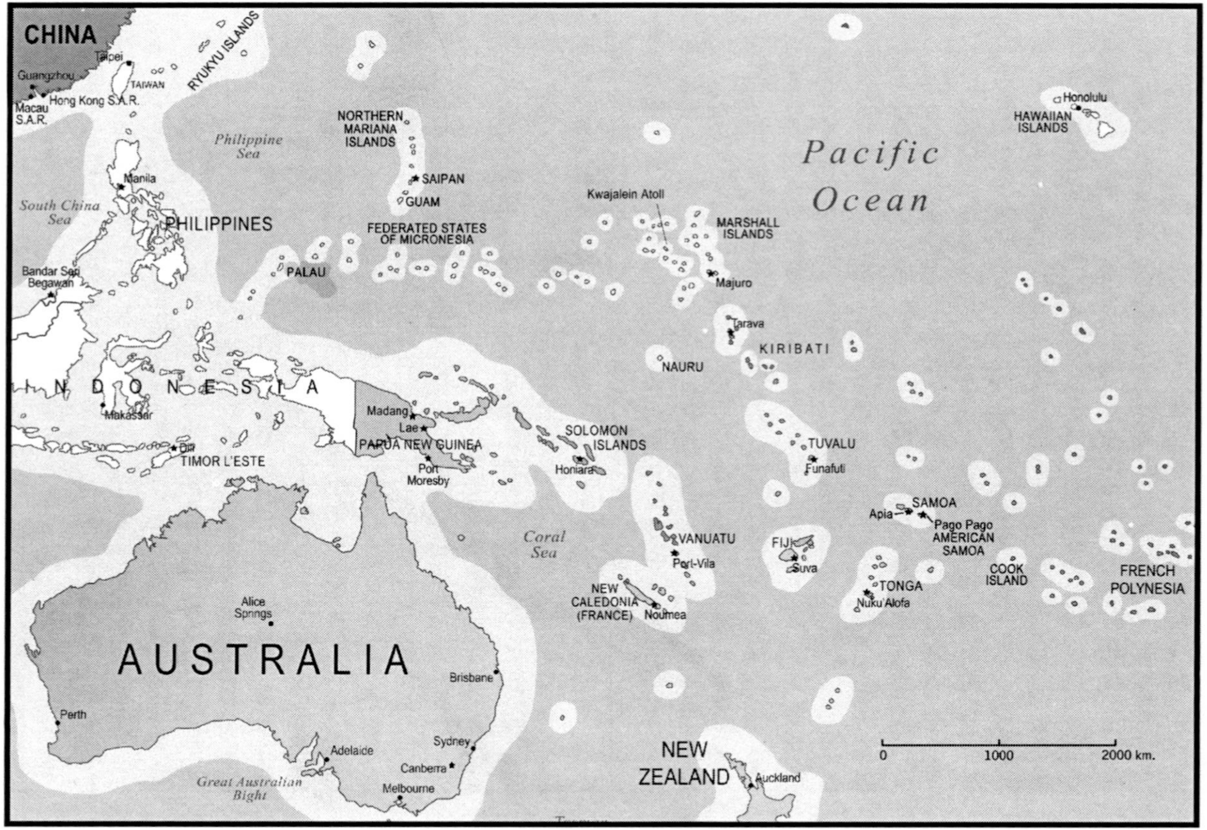

CHAPTER TWO
TREASURE ISLANDS

There is nothing wrong or unusual about the food at Ang's Chinese restaurant. In fact, the roast duck served there is excellent and the *Lonely Planet* travel guide assures you that its hot-and-sour soup is special. It is just the way the place looks. The yard is surrounded by high walls with razor wire and surveillance cameras. Two security guards watch the entrance and open the sliding iron gate only if customers, in their vehicle, appear to be genuinely wanting to have just a meal. Having satisfied the guards and parked the car inside the gate, lunch or dinner guests are met by another steel door guarded by more watchmen. They will not only shut the door but lock it once the guests are in the actual restaurant building. Then they may enjoy Ang's oriental fare in peace.

Welcome to Port Moresby, the capital of Papua New Guinea—and, according to a 2005 survey by the Economist Intelligence Unit, the worst place to live among 130 world capitals and major cities. An Australian-funded report seems to confirm this grim assessment. Two-thirds of all households were victims of crime in the first five months of 2005, and weapons were used in just over half of these instances. The murder rate is three times that of Moscow and 23 times higher than in London. On a visit back to Papua New Guinea in 2005, Rowan Callick, a British journalist who was based there for eleven years following independence from Australia in 1975, invited ten former local colleagues—printers, typists, drivers—out for a meal. He asked them how many had been robbed at gunpoint. Eight put their hands up.

The hotel where I stayed in Port Moresby, the Crown Plaza, perched on a hill overlooking the city centre, had three armed guards outside the front gate, plus two huge German shepherd dogs. And then, needless to say, a high wall with razor wire, surveillance cameras and powerful spotlights at night. I was advised not to venture out on foot even in broad daylight. And this was in one of the poshest areas in central Port Moresby. Founded in the 1870s as a trading post by Captain John Moresby, a British naval officer who explored the coast of New Guinea, it was named after its founder. Once a pretty town with a fine natural harbour, it has become a law and order nightmare where no one is safe.

Papua New Guinea's notorious *raskols*—Pidgin English for rascals—are everywhere. They are gangs of young men for whom crime has become a way of life. Having moved into Port Moresby from the highlands or elsewhere in the countryside, they end up in shantytowns and suburbs where unemployment rates hover between 70 and 90 per cent. And they were born into a culture where tribal warfare, vendettas and violence are deeply ingrained. Add the availability of firearms in urban areas, and it is not surprising that Port Moresby's homes resemble top security prisons.

It is also not difficult to understand why so many Australians—citizens of the former colonial power— and other Western expatriates have left or are leaving. At independence in 1975, there were nearly 50,000 non-citizens in the country. Now only a few thousand Australians, Britons and Germans remain. But, as the chatter in Ang's restaurant indicated, newly-arrived mainland Chinese are replacing them as businessmen, contractors and importers-exporters. Jerry Singirok, a former Papua New Guinea Defence Force commander, wrote in a local newspaper in 2005: "Australia has always considered Papua New Guinea as its backyard [but] since 2000, Papua New Guinea has increased its bilateral relations with China in areas of trade, investment and the military...China is here to stay."

Many are indeed here to stay permanently. According to various estimates, there could be anywhere between 10,000 and 30,000 Chinese citizens in the country. Many of them are here illegally, but Papua New Guinea passports, and therefore citizenship, are not difficult to obtain. Corruption is endemic at all levels in the government and local administration.

And aid from China comes in handy when countries such as Australia threaten to cut their assistance because of allegations of corruption, nepotism and abuse of power. "China's rising status as an economic power is becoming an important pillar for developing countries like Papua New Guinea," Tarcy Eli, a high-ranking foreign ministry official, said at China's national day celebrations on October 1, 2005. China's voice at the United Nations, he said, was "one for the developing world."

And according to Singirok: "Covertly, major powers are cautious and apprehensive about China's greater role in the region in terms of trading and military." That may be so, but it would be hard to lure anyone from those "major powers" to work, let alone settle, in Port Moresby. Unless they are prepared to stay behind high walls with razor wire, and security guards with guns and ferocious dogs by day as well as by night. As even the *Lonely Planet* points out, "the *raskols* are not strictly nocturnal."

I spent no more than four days in Port Moresby, but it was enough to get a feel for the place, and the dangers that seemed to be lurking around almost every corner. Steve Marshall, a young New Zealander who then worked there as the local correspondent for the Australian Broadcasting Corporation, picked me up from my hotel and drove me around town and its suburbs. The roads, traffic signs and even some suburban villas could have been transplanted from rural Australia. But there was graffiti everywhere, many roads were potholed and badly maintained, houses were fortified—and it was not safe to stop anywhere. At first, Steve had come to Port Moresby together with his girlfriend, but, after a while, she moved to safety in Brisbane. Steve flew down there almost every weekend to see her—and to live a normal life for a few days. He kindly let me go through his archives of press clippings, and we had lunch at Ang's Chinese restaurant as well as dinner at the Royal Papua Yacht Club, a colonial relic down by the harbour where expatriates and wealthy locals sipped drinks and ate Western-style pub food—behind high walls and with armed guards at the gate. I felt like a silly Western expatriate on an excursion in a developing nation. But there was no choice as even the staff at my hotel told me not to venture out alone.

But all that did not seem to deter Papua New Guinea's new Chinese migrants and settlers. Papua New Guinea, with its vast reserves of minerals, timber, oil and gas has attracted not only private businessmen but Chinese state enterprises as well. In the mid-1990s, only 0.5 per cent of Papua New Guinea's log exports went to China. Today it is 80 per cent. In the 1990s New Guinea's mining sector was dominated mainly by Australian but also British and Canadian companies. Today, China is moving in there as well. Papua New Guinea has nickel, cobalt, copper and, in the highlands, even gold. In 2003, the China Metallurgical Group became the majority shareholder of Ramu NiCo, which owns a nickel mine near Madang, a town on the northeastern coast of the country. As Geoffrey York, a Canadian journalist, wrote in the January 2, 2009 issue of the daily *Globe and Mail*: "With a planned investment of 1.4 billion US dollars and an expected lifespan of 20 to 40 years, Ramu is one of the biggest mining projects China has ever attempted overseas. And China Metallurgical is determined to do it right."

A red Chinese banner flies over the tallest new building in Madang. This is the headquarters of Ramu NiCo, which has financed some construction projects and built a bridge over one of the rivers in the area. But it has not done everything right. In early 2007, Papua New Guinea's labour minister, David Tibu, paid a surprise visit to the mine. He found that the local workers were treated like slaves. They were paid less than three US dollars a day and given tins of fish as compensation for overtime work. Christianity is strong in the area, but the workers were not allowed to go to church on Sundays. When they went anyway, the company deducted a day's work from their pay. The canteen where the workers ate was "not fit for pigs," the minister declared, and the toilets were filthy. Tibu's findings made the headlines of the country's newspapers—and prompted the Chinese to embark on a vigorous PR drive. The Chinese-owned company pledged to set aside millions of dollars to build clinics, schools and churches, and to support rugby and basketball teams, local farmers and festivals.

But many villagers were still unhappy when York of the *Globe and Mail* visited the site in late 2008: "Tensions have sometimes erupted into violence. In August, a Chinese security officer was badly injured in a struggle with protesting villagers near the nickel refinery site, about two hours by boat from Madang. Guards still roam around the site, protecting the workers from further attacks by the landowners." The main problem seems to be that the natives consider that the land in and around the site belongs to traditional landowners, while the Chinese do not have any real concept of private land ownership. York quoted a local radio journalist in Madang as saying that, "the Chinese have a system where everything is owned by the government, and the government tells you what to do. Their deal for the Ramu project is on a government-to-government basis. The Chinese don't understand the value of land to the people."

Another controversy, according to York, is over the Chinese company's failure to obtain legal work permits for many of its technicians and engineers. In November 2008, police arrested 213 Chinese employees of the Ramu mine for having entered the country on improper permits. The company was hit with a 720,000 US dollar fine for breaching labour laws and blasted in the national media, which accused it of importing Chinese workers for jobs that locals could do, York wrote in his investigative piece on the controversial mining project.

It was not the first time Chinese nationals were involved in a document forgery in the country. In 2000, it was revealed that officers from Papua New Guinea's Foreign Affairs Department were involved in a major passport scam together with some non-citizens. In a "Special Brief" for the Foreign Minister—stamped "secret" and dated November 2000—the country's National Intelligence Organisation, NIO, stated that it had "written literally dozens of briefs on various Papua New Guinea scams involving human smuggling, phoney entry permits, and false passports." But none of these scams could operate without the compliance of corrupt bureaucrats, the NIO concluded. The brief went on to name two government officials who had helped not only Chinese but also Sri Lankans, other Asians and even Africans obtain Papua New Guinea passports, which were then used to stay in the country, or travel on to Australia or New Zealand.

Chinese-owned shops and small restaurants have sprung up all over Papua New Guinea by migrants using false passports and work permits, and often—as in the Russian Far East—using locals as fronts. In Madang, and the capital Port Moresby, nearly half of the fast-food outlets and shops are owned by newly arrived Chinese migrants. The Papuans are not happy about this, and more angry voices could be heard when, on July 22nd, 2005, the daily *Post Courier* reported that Chinese shop owners sent their earnings to foreign banks, and that little money stayed in the country.

Resentment of the migrants is growing. In September 2007, police fired warning shots at local people who were looting and ransacking Chinese-owned businesses in Mount Hagen in the Western Highlands, the country's third largest city after Port Moresby and the coastal town of Lae. "Even schoolchildren were reportedly seen running away with clothing, food and kitchenware," the British Broadcasting Corporation reported on September 21. Several shops and warehouses were burnt to the ground and the gangs of looters hit back at the police with a barrage of stones.

In May 2009, anti-Chinese riots once again rocked Papua New Guinea. It began at the Ramu nickel mine, where the Chinese owners had actually launched a PR campaign to improve their image. A fight erupted between Papuan and Chinese workers at the site, three Chinese were injured in the melee and 70 Papuans charged with being responsible for the fighting. A few days later, a protest march was held in Port Moresby to demand that the government curb the "immigration of Asians"—a general term that refers mainly to people from China. Chinese-owned shops were ransacked and looted, veteran Papua new Guinea watcher Rowan Callick reported in the May 23, 2009 issue of *The Australian*: "Fast-food outlets known as 'tucker boxes' and other small businesses run by Asians were swiftly closed down in Port Moresby and other cities as the protests spread. Such retail operations have typically provided the main channel for Papua New Guineans to set up in business. But they have been largely taken over in recent years by Asian operators with access to much cheaper products."

The rioting, Callick reported, spread first to the country's second city, Lae, and then to Madang and through the Highlands, to Kainantu, Goroka, Wabag and Mount Hagen: "Prices for basic foodstuffs soared as town stores were closed for two days." At least three looters were shot dead during the riots, while a fourth looter was trampled to death in a stampede.

And it is not only native Papuans who have reacted against the influx of newcomers from China. Papua New Guinea actually has one of the oldest Chinese communities in the Pacific. In the late 19th century, the island of New Guinea was divided between the Netherlands, which controlled the western half, Germany which had made the northeastern quarter its colony, and Britain, which from Australia ruled the southeastern part called Papua. It was an artificial, colonial division where borders were straight lines on the map drawn up in Europe.

Britain and the Netherlands were not keen on encouraging Chinese immigration, but the Germans imported hundreds of Cantonese-speaking Chinese workers from the southern province of Guangdong each year to work on tobacco and coconut plantations, and as cooks or domestic servants for German officials and entrepreneurs. Some Chinese later became mechanics, carpenters and tailors required in the colonial economy. When World War I broke out in Europe in 1914, British-Australian forces took over the German colony. Some Chinese were repatriated and restrictions were imposed on those who remained. But many were not sent back to China, and some moved to other parts of the now combined territory of Papua New Guinea. In the late 1940s, after World War II, many Chinese came to play an important role as middlemen servicing the needs of the growing urban population. By then Britain had handed over the territory to Australia, which had become more of an independent nation.

About 3,000 Chinese and part-Chinese lived in Papua New Guinea before independence in 1975. But many Chinese were worried about their future in a Papuan-ruled nation, and it was even unclear if they were going to be given Papua New Guinean citizenship. As a consequence, most of them emigrated to Australia and more moved out when *raskol* violence became a problem in the 1990s. But a thousand or so stayed behind, and one of those of mixed blood, Julius Chan, served as the country's prime minister in 1980-82 and again in 1994-97. They were, however, a tiny minority in a country of 6.3 million people. Then came the newcomers.

There is a wide gap between them and the Chinese who have been there for generations. Christine Inglis of the University of Sydney says that "'local' and 'overseas' Chinese are distinguished by more than birthplace and period of settlement. A cultural and social divide separates the locally born Cantonese speakers, who have been extensively influenced by contacts with Australians and other Europeans, from the new arrivals, few of whom speak Cantonese and have much closer links with traditional Chinese culture." Many Chinese old-timers also feel closer to the Republic of China, or Taiwan, than the communist-ruled People's Republic of China.

That divide reflects a broader issue in the Pacific: rivalry between mainland China and Taiwan. Less than about two dozen countries recognise Taipei as the legitimate government of China—and six of them are small Pacific island nations: Kiribati, Nauru, the Marshall Islands, Palau, Tuvalu and the Solomon Islands. The rest are a few African and Latin American states, and island nations in the Caribbean. For Taiwan, the fact that it is recognised by some countries is essential to prove its status as a separate country, and not just an island claimed by the mainland.

Taipei's efforts to get official diplomatic support for "the Republic of China" therefore always comes with generous offers of aid, something that the impoverished island-countries of the Pacific badly need. Beijing has adopted similar tactics to deny Taiwan recognition. China's aid to the Pacific's largest and most resource-rich state, Papua New Guinea, is now second only to that of Australia, and Beijing has funded government buildings in Vanuatu, Samoa and the Cook Islands, and new sports stadiums for Fiji, Samoa, Kiribati and the Federated States of Micronesia. China now has more diplomats in the region than any other country and China also provides military assistance to the few Pacific states that maintain forces—Fiji, Tonga, Vanuatu and Papua

New Guinea. Officers from those countries are being trained at China's National Defence Academy in Beijing, and in 2005 China and Papua New Guinea agreed to exchange military attachés. China has also helped with equipment, computer systems, tents, uniforms, gymnasiums and other supplies, martial arts trainers and interpreters.

But there is also something bigger going on here. While the attention of the United States after the September 11, 2001 terrorist attacks in New York and Washington became focused on Afghanistan and Iraq, China began to gain even more influence in what had long been regarded as America's home turf, the Pacific. Some analysts have even suggested that the ocean is becoming the venue for a new Cold War where the United States and China compete for client states and economic and strategic advantage. The vast Pacific Ocean is economically important as it covers some of the world's richest fishing grounds, and, whoever controls the Pacific also controls vital shipping lanes between the Asian and American continents, some of the busiest in the world.

America's interest in the region began when the frontiers of the United States reached the Pacific Ocean in the mid-19th century. California was bought—and conquered—from Mexico, and, in 1867, the United States purchased Alaska from the Russian Empire, sealing American control over most of non-Latin America except British North America, as Canada was then known. But American expansion did not stop at the shores of the Pacific. In 1893, American and European businessmen overthrew the king of the Hawaiian Islands, which were annexed five years later and, in 1900, officially became a US territory. In 1959, it was made the 50th state of the United States.

The Spanish-American War in 1898 brought the United States closer to the Asian mainland. In the Pacific, Spain was forced to cede the Philippines and Guam to the United States, which then, in effect, became an Asian colonial power. Since then, American supremacy in the Pacific Ocean has been challenged only by Japan in the 1930s and 1940s, and, more recently, by China.

Benjamin Reilly, a senior lecturer at the Australian National University in Canberra, believes that China is expanding its influence over the Pacific with "the long-term aim of challenging the United States as the prime mover in the Pacific. It can no longer be taken for granted that Oceania will remain a relatively benign 'American Lake'." The very weakness of Pacific island states makes them vulnerable as a strategic resource for China, Reilly argues.

Taiwan's interests in the Pacific are clear and relatively narrow. Besides its need for diplomatic recognition, it also has economic interests in the Pacific. Its fishing fleets are some of the largest in the region, operating across central and western Pacific.

Beijing, on the other hand, has more far-reaching interests in the Pacific, says Mohan Malik, an Indian-born China analyst at the Asia Pacific Centre for Security Studies in Honolulu: "In the short term, it wants to isolate Taiwan in the international community. But in the medium and longer term its goal is to challenge and eventually displace the United States as the guardian and protector of the Pacific."

Other analysts may describe America's role in the Pacific as a colonial power rather than a benefactor, but Mailk's views are those of most US-based commentators. Malik also believes that Beijing wants to emerge as a major Pacific-region aid donor and economic partner, which would undermine the influence of the United States in the region and Oceania's special ties with Washington. He also argues that increased Chinese tourism and emigration are part of Beijing's strategy of "economic penetration of Oceania." In recent years, thousands of Chinese have settled not only in Papua New Guinea but all over the Pacific where they are also running grocery stores, restaurants and other small businesses. The numbers may not be significant in a global context, but Chinese migration to these Pacific states, which with the exception of Papua New Guinea have tiny populations, is bound to upset traditional ethnic and economic patterns.

And with the realisation of China's ambition to develop a blue-water navy capable of sailing the oceans of the world, which it now lacks, would be an increase of its interest in the Pacific. Today, despite recent developments, the region is not at the top of Beijing's list of security priorities. Taiwan and the Spratly Islands in the South China Sea figure much more prominently. But China has seen how Japan and other countries have historically used the Pacific Islands to build their Pacific empires. In the 19th century, the region was effectively divided between Britain, France and Germany. A year after the United States had seized Hawaii and acquired Guam and the Philippines from Spain, the islands of Samoa were divided between the United States and Germany.

After World War I, Japan expanded into the Pacific as it took over the German colonies of the Marshall Islands, the Northern Marianas, Palau and the Carolines, now Micronesia—small islands but with vast areas of ocean under their jurisdiction. Japan's expansion into the Pacific Ocean eventually led to war with the United States, when Japanese forces attacked Hawaii's Pearl Harbour on December 7, 1941. Although there is no evidence that China will seek to expand its influence by waging war, it seems inevitable that its economic, political and strategic interests in the region will clash with those of the United States in the longer term. Apart from being preoccupied with its Middle Eastern imbroglio, it is also clear how much Washington needs Beijing's support there and with issues such as North Korea. The United States has even pulled out diplomats from the Pacific and downgraded its presence in the region. This has created a vacuum that China is taking full advantage of.

The islands of Melanesia have always been vulnerable to outside penetration as they have no real concept of nationhood. More than 800 languages are spoken in Papua New Guinea and the 192,000 inhabitants of the much smaller Vanuatu speak 114 different languages. When the Europeans first arrived in the West Pacific in the 17th and 18th centuries, they saw them as "new" lands. The name New Guinea was coined in 1545 by the Spanish explorer Ortiz Retes, while attempting to return from the Moluccas in today's Indonesia to Mexico. The people he saw reminded him of those of the Guinea coast of Africa, so it became "New Guinea."

The first European who sighted New Caledonia, now a French overseas territory, was British Captain James Cook. He named the island New Caledonia because its pine-clad ridges reminded him of Scotland, Caledonia being the Latin name given by the Romans to the land on the northern tip of the British Isles. When he spotted an archipelago to the northeast, he named them the New Hebrides after the islands off the coast of Scotland. The New Hebrides has now become Vanuatu, but most of the old names remain. In New Guinea, there are the provinces of West and East New Britain, and New Ireland. The addition "Papua" to the name of the country is derived from a Malay word describing the frizzy Melanesian hair. And then, of course, there is New Zealand, originally Polynesian and not Melanesian, which the Dutch explorer Abel Tasman sighted in 1642. Why Dutch cartographers named the mountainous island after the flat Dutch province of Zeeland is a mystery, but the name stuck and was Anglicised to New Zealand by Captain Cook.

And colonisation was often a very brutal experience. The missionaries, who arrived in the mid- and late 19th century, condemned indigenous cultures as "pagan" and often ran roughshod over the local population. Measles, gonorrhoea, syphilis and smallpox came with the European sailors, and unscrupulous traders kidnapped the natives and sold them to plantations in Queensland, Australia. This practice, called "blackbirding," continued throughout the 19th century, and almost entirely depleted the populations of many of the islands in this "new" world.

An even more incongruous name than New Guinea or New Caledonia is the Solomon Islands, the largest island nation in Melanesia outside Papua New Guinea. Spanish explorer Alvaro de Mendana de Neira was the first European to land there. He set out from Peru with two ships in 1567 with about 150 sailors, soldiers, priests and slaves on board to seek for the legendary Isles of Solomon, where the Biblical king Solomon was supposed to have hidden his treasures. These islands were also said to have been visited by the Incas of South America. Why, and how, Solomon would have transported his gold as far away as the Pacific was never explained, but it was at the time believed that those treasure islands were located somewhere west of South America.

De Mendana never found any gold, but he named the islands he saw Santa Isabel, Guadalcanal, Malaita and San Cristobal—names that were completely alien to the native population. The Spanish-named islands, collectively known as the Solomons, were declared a British protectorate in 1893, and became independent in 1978. But the Queen of Britain is still the head of state of the Solomon Islands, as she is of Papua New Guinea and, of course, Australia, New Zealand, Canada, Jamaica, and some other former British possessions.

After four rather harrowing days in Papua New Guinea, I flew to the Solomons. Its tiny capital, Honiara, was far more relaxed than Port Moresby. Honiara stretches for a few kilometres along Mendana Avenue, its only major road and aptly named after the first European visitor to the islands. The hotel where I stayed was also named after the Spanish explorer and called The Kitano Mendana. It was right on the waterfront, with a fresh breeze flowing in from the sea. The rest of the town had a fairly shabby look to it although there were a few cafés, some shops—and a Chinatown. And its government does recognise Taiwan, not China.

I was taken on a tour of Honiara's Chinatown by Anna Powles, a New Zealand academic whose grandfather, Guy Powles, was the last New Zealand governor of Samoa, before it became independent in 1962. He had also commanded the New Zealand artillery regiment in the South Pacific at Guadalcanal in the Solomons, and in New Caledonia during World War II, which saw heavy fighting in the region between Japanese and Allied Western forces. The old battle sites from the war have become tourist attractions, to the extent that the Solomon Islands get any tourists. I did not encounter many during my stay on the islands.

We walked down Mendana Avenue, past rows of rather ugly shophouses, and across the bridge on the Mataniko River. And there it was: a cluster of Chinese-owned general stores selling all kinds of foodstuff and consumer goods: soap, cloth, pots and pans, instant noodles, chips, corned beef, soft drinks, beer, tools and children's toys. The sales assistants were mostly locals, and the owners—all Chinese—were seated on high beachguard-style chairs, overlooking their stores and collecting money from the customers. It was a rather provocative scene and I was left to wonder if it had not been better for the Chinese store-owners to be a bit more considerate and supervise from the floor rather than from above, especially when the racial differences were so obvious: fair-skinned Chinese versus black Melanesians.

They should have every reason to be cautious, and perhaps more discreet. The Solomons have only about half a million people but it is a deeply divided, violent society. In the late 1990s, ethnic tension between people from different islands erupted into violent clashes. The capital Honiara is located on Guadalcanal, the richest of the islands. After independence, it began to attract migrants from the poorer nearby island of Malaita, which the tribes of Guadalcanal resented. In 1999, a local militia that styled itself as the Guadalcanal Revolutionary Army began to terrorise Malaitian settlers, who responded by forming the Malaitan Eagle Force. Both groups were armed with guns as well as machetes and axes, and were equally brutal.

Hundreds of people died in the fighting, and it did not end until Australia and New Zealand, in October 2000, managed to mediate a settlement between the two forces. The Solomons, like Papua New Guinea, is a tribal society with little or no national cohesion. The *lingua franca* in both countries—and in nearby Vanuatu—is Pidgin, a bastardised kind of primitive English that was first introduced by European traders, who treated the natives as children and spoke to them in a descriptive, child-like language. For instance, a sign outside a public lavatory in Papua New Guinea said "Do not misuse the toilet," followed by "No kan bagarapim haus pek-pek" in Pidgin, or, literally, "no can bugger up house pee-pee." A crown prince would be "Nambawan pikinini blong King mo Kwin" ("Number one pickaninny belong King more Queen"), a grand piano "bigfela bokis yu kilim emi singout" ("big fellow box, you hit it, it sings out") and a violin "Smal sista blong bigfala bokis i krae" ("small sister belong big fellow box it cries"). It may sound like gibberish to most outsiders, but the fact that there is a common language in these ethnically divided societies has contributed to a sense of nationhood, albeit weak and fragile.

And the tension in Solomon Islands never fully died down. In July 2003, Australian and Pacific Island troops arrived under the auspices of the Regional Assistance Mission to the Solomon Islands, or RAMSI. Since that time, the Solomon Islands have been considered by many a failed state, unable to solve it own problems and dependent entirely on outside forces to maintain law and order. However, many would argue that Australia's intervention in the Solomon Islands and elsewhere in the Pacific is not entirely altruistic. Australia, too has, superpower ambitions, at least in the Asia-Pacific region. On several occasions, Australia has also intervened in East Timor mainly to protect its own economic and security interests. Australia was the only Western power that recognised the 1976 Indonesian annexation of the former Portuguese colony—which Indonesia had invaded in 1975. Australia's main interests at that time were oil and gas deposits in the sea between its northern coast and the island of Timor, and to prevent a left-wing government from taking over East Timor. Those interests have not changed over the years—and Australia's role in the Pacific is also motivated by a desire to control smaller and weaker, neighbouring island nations.

On the other hand, the Solomons have been heavily exploited by unscrupulous logging companies, mainly from Malaysia but also from South Korea and some other countries. Around 80 per cent of the Solomon Islands; 27,540 square kilometres are—or until recently were—covered with tropical rainforest. Since the early 1990s, the timber industry has been a significant sector in the economy, contributing 20 per cent of government revenues annually, and more than 50 per cent of export revenues. Laws have been enacted to regulate the logging industry, but rampant corruption has rendered those restrictions meaningless.

Malaysian companies began raping the forests of the Solomon Islands and defrauding the people there to the extent that alarm bells sounded even at home in Malaysia. In 1996, in an unprecedented move, the then Malaysian deputy Prime Minister—and now opposition leader—Anwar Ibrahim called on Malaysian companies to be sensitive to environmental issues and not to over-log. But no one was prepared to listen. And a 2005 report commissioned by the Solomon Islands government found that large amounts of tax had not been paid by the logging companies, as they routinely bribed local politicians to obtain unlawful "exemptions." Vast quantities of logs continue to be shipped out of the country.

An NGO, the Christian Care Centre, published an even more damning report in 2007. Malaysian loggers were found to be involved in horrific sexual abuse of village children as well. The children were raped, sold into marriage and used for pornography, and, according to the report, they "ranged from age 11 through to 19, with most children being aged 13 to 15 years…Most of the perpetrators were foreign loggers…[and] child prostitution was reported in every village visited." Also of concern, the report went on, was the use of children and young boys to arrange girls or carry messages in exchange for money or alcohol. Such messengers were known as "Solair"— named after the Solomons' national airline.

Most loggers from Malaysia were ethnic Chinese, which inevitably gave rise to anti-Chinese sentiments in the Solomons. It also meant that any Chinese was seen as an exploiter with little or no concern for local sensibilities, whether he was an ordinary local shopkeeper or someone who raped children. About 2,000 of Honiara's 50,000 inhabitants are ethnic Chinese, and most of them have been living there peacefully for generations. Some moved there from New Guinea in the early 20th century, while others came direct from China and Australia. During the colonial era, they worked as labourers, cooks and laundry boys for British administrators and plantation owners. Over the years, they worked hard and managed to set up retail stores and other businesses. Today, they dominate both wholesale and retail trade in Honiara. And, since the 1990s, new settlers have arrived from mainland China. The Solomons were ripe for another ethnic explosion.

In April 2006, a year after my visit to the islands, long-simmering discontent with the economically more powerful Chinese—old-timers as well as newly arrived Chinese from Malaysia and even mainland China—erupted into violent riots. The trigger was allegations that the newly elected Prime Minister Snyder Rini had used bribes from Chinese businessmen to buy votes of members of Parliament.

Protesters armed with knives and axes threatened to destroy the entire capital unless Rini stepped down. Inevitably, the Chinese were the main targets and victims of the riots. Honiara's Chinatown was almost levelled following looting and arson. The rioters also attacked the Pacific Casino on the waterfront between downtown Honiara and the airport, which was renowned for Chinese—in this case Taiwanese—money-laundering.

But many victims were from the mainland, and since Taiwan, not China, has an embassy in Honiara, they appealed to China's mission in Port Moresby for help. Beijing sent four chartered planes to evacuate several hundred of its citizens, and 21 from Hong Kong. They were airlifted to Port Moresby, and then on to Guangzhou in China.

Australia, New Zealand and Fiji sent extra troops to the Solomons to help restore peace, and the Solomon Islands Governor-General, Sir Nathaniel Waena, the local representative of the Queen of Britain, officially apologised to the Chinese community. He also appealed to those who had left to return if they still regarded the islands as their home. Rini was forced to resign.

The Taiwanese denied any political interference in the Solomons, but it is undeniable that "check-book diplomacy" by Taiwan as well as mainland China has fuelled corruption not only in the Solomons but all over the Pacific. Taiwan is a major donor to the Solomon Islands government, which has received millions of dollars in aid for rural development projects, educational scholarships and urban infrastructure development. The Taiwan government has funded a hospital and an agricultural research station in Honiara, staffed partly by Taiwanese personnel. In 2007, 20 Solomon Islands policemen were trained in Taipei, and Taiwan is becoming more involved in the country's security services, perhaps to keep an eye on newly arrived migrants from mainland China.

On the seedier side was the now destroyed Pacific Casino, which was also where Robert Goh, a wealthy local Chinese businessman, had his office. He once served as advisor to Rini's predecessor as prime minister, Allan Kemakeza, whose administration was tainted by corruption allegations. Kemakeza was also very close to other ethnic Chinese businessmen. Among them was Thomas, or 'Tommy' Chan, father of Laurie Chan, Foreign Minister in the Kemakeza government. Tommy Chan owned the Honiara Hotel in Chinatown, where Rini and his followers camped in the run up to the elections. Chan was also the president of a group of influential parliamentarians called the Association of Independent Members of Parliament, to which Rini belonged.

Even if official ties with Taiwan are stronger than with China, local Solomon Islanders seldom comprehend the difference between the "two Chinas." Even the Malaysian loggers are seen as belonging to the same group of "outsiders" who have come to dominate all economic aspects of their country—and to interfere in local politics. Asians have earned a bad name in the Solomon Islands, but what is the solution? Shortly after the April 2006 riots, Solomon Islands Labour Party leader Joses Tuhanuku told the Australian daily newspaper *The Australian* that the ethnic crisis in 2006 was much worse than the clashes between the Guadalcanal Revolutionary Army and the Malaitan Eagle Force in 1999-2000: "People feel that they have lost their country. The Solomon Islands are no longer in the hands of Solomon Islanders; it is now in the hands of the Chinese who control the economic life of the country, and now they are taking over the political life of the country."

Tuhanuku's sentiments were shared by many other Solomon Islanders. Also commenting on the riots in an article in the local newspaper, the *Solomon Star*, veteran civil servant George Manimu observed that people have long resented their leaders' giving preferential treatment to foreigners, especially Asians, when it came to trade, logging, and fisheries. "Business areas, often referred to as reserved for nationals, have also become dominated by Asian entrepreneurs," Manimu wrote. "The actions of the people (during the riots), although criminal, reflect the release of bottled up frustrations and anger that they could not contain any longer." As is the case in Port Moresby, there is widespread poverty and unemployment among young people, who make up most of the population in both places. There are no *raskols* in Honiara, but groups of restless young men can be seen loitering in the streets. It takes very little to ignite a riot.

The rivalry between China and Taiwan—and the influx of Chinese businessmen and settlers to the Pacific region—is bound to result in more riots similar to those in Honiara in April 2006. And then there could perhaps be an even more direct Chinese intervention than just airlifting nationals, as was done after the Honiara riots. As soon as the evacuees had been repatriated, Chinese President Hu Jintao and Prime Minister Wen Jiabao instructed the Foreign Ministry in Beijing to "take measures to ensure the safety of Chinese nationals" in the Solomon Islands. In 2003 and 2006, Australian-led forces restored law and order, but what if China decides to send troops to protect its citizens and interests in the region?

As Jerry Singirok, the former Papua New Guinea commander, said as early as 2005: "China is here to stay." The mineral resources and vast forest reserves of Melanesia are too high a price to give up. And then there are long-term strategic considerations, which China's security planners would be most unwilling to reconsider only because of some anti-Chinese riots in the Solomons or law and order problems in Papua New Guinea.

CHAPTER THREE
PEARLS OF THE PACIFIC

Two buildings stand out on Beach Road, the main street through Samoa's capital Apia. Near the town's landmark clock tower is Chan Mow's shopping centre, an imposing old building first opened as Burns Philp department store in 1934. Across the road and a green park towers the modern, seven-storey Government Building, erected in 1994 with a multi-million dollar interest free loan from the People's Republic of China. The former represents the economic power of Samoa's old Chinese; the latter the growing influence of China in this Polynesian nation of 185,000 people. Samoa has a small but prosperous Chinese community that dates back to pre-World War I days—and Samoa has had diplomatic ties with Beijing since November 6,1975, the first of the Pacific islands to recognise the People's Republic of China after Fiji, which established relations with Beijing a day ahead, on November 5.

When Chan Mow took over the shopping centre in the mid-1990s, a year before he died, he was one of the richest men in the country. But his life story also reflects the discrimination the Chinese had to endure when Samoa was ruled by colonial powers. The Germans, who arrived at the turn of the last century, were the first outsiders to take possession of the islands and they imported labour from China to work on coconut plantations and as domestic servants. In total, over 6,000 Chinese left for Samoa between 1903 and 1913, most of them from the southern provinces of Guangdong and Fujian. The voyages to Samoa took about three weeks, with no ports of call along the way. It was an arduous journey with appalling conditions on the ships. A Chinese labourer later recalled:

"Life on-board the ship was monotonous. Long hours were spent simply day-dreaming. No typhoons buffeted the ship. No sightings of playful dolphins nor whales, mammoth denizens of the deep. Not even that of a passing freighter. Crowded conditions prevailed. The men slept on double and triple-decker bunk beds in the hot and stuffy hold of the ship. Ventilation was poor, lighting dim, comforts minimal and sometimes the stench overpowering from the vomit of the seasick."

Many died on their way to Samoa, and those who survived the journey soon discovered that their employers did not adhere to the terms of contracts they had agreed upon while recruiting workers in China. Samoa was not the tropical paradise they had seen on posters in Guangdong and Fujian. Working conditions on the plantations were harsh, and, as Samoan historian Featuna'i Ben Liuaana put it, "to make matters worse, the German government sanctioned flogging for the most minute misconduct, at twenty lashes each, once a week, before a government official, as if his presence made it less barbaric."

Then, in 1914, World War I broke out and New Zealand occupied the islands. Most Germans and Chinese were repatriated to their respective countries, but more than 800 Chinese stayed on in Samoa. All of them were men and, in 1921, the New Zealand authorities introduced a law prohibiting marriages between Chinese and Samoans. But many Chinese nevertheless lived together with Samoan women, and had children. So in 1931, the colonial power made it illegal for Chinese even to enter Samoan houses, and Samoan women entering the homes of labourers. The Samoan race had to be kept "pure" and the authorities must contain what a New Zealand official called "the yellow taint which was coming down through the Pacific."

But labour was still needed in Samoa, and between 1920 and 1934, New Zealand arranged for eight shipments from China carrying 3,116 men. The last shipment included Chinese from Taishan, or Toishan, in Guangdong province, a district that at the time saw massive emigration because of severe poverty. Most of the Toishan migrants ended up in New York, but those who went to Samoa were lured into signing contracts which once again did not tell the whole truth. Nancy W.Y. Tom wrote, in her 1986 study *The Chinese in Western Samoa, 1875-1985: The Dragon Came From Afar*, that the agents "wove an appealing tale of happy and well-fed Chinese in the islands accompanied by pretty brown-skinned belles clutching almond-eyed babies in their arms relaxing under the swaying fronds of stately coconut palms."

The reality was entirely different, and the newly arrived Chinese suffered not only from inhuman working conditions but also from the terror of their own criminal gangs, secret societies which had followed the labourers to the islands. The gangs extorted "protection money" from the labourers, and threatened to beat those who refused to pay. They also imported opium from China, sometimes via Hawaii, where many more Chinese had settled. A huge opium addiction problem afflicted the Chinese in Samoa. The importation of opium was made illegal, but that only led to the emergence of a thriving black market. And the smugglers were not only Chinese; many New Zealanders also brought in opium on ships from China. With little else to do, many Chinese spent their free time, when they had any, gambling in dens run by criminal gangs. The gambling trapped many Chinese in debt, while others became drug addicts.

Nearly all Chinese were repatriated after World War II, and, in September 1948, the last Chinese repatriates were literally dragged onto the ships despite protests by Samoan families and friends, leaving behind spouses and children. But some with Samoan families managed to stay behind. Chan Mow was one of them. He had arrived in Samoa in 1934 with nothing and, as Ron Crocombe, the world's leading expert on the Pacific, wrote in his study of Asians in the region, "began as a groundsman and plantation labourer, working as a share-cropper till late at night, and, on Sundays, selling pork from his bicycle." He managed to save enough money to open a restaurant, grocery, farm, bakery and wholesale business—and, eventually, Samoa's main shopping centre.

At his funeral in 1996, Apia was brought to a standstill. Thousands of mourners showed up, among them Samoa's Head of State, Malietoa Tanumafili II, Prime Minister Tofilau Eti Alesana and his entire cabinet as well as leaders of the political opposition. The requiem mass—Chan Mow was a Roman Catholic—was celebrated by Cardinal Pio Taofinu'u. And, as a testimony to the futility of the old, colonial law banning sexual relationships between Chinese and Samoans, he left behind a Samoan wife, 13 children, 37 grandchildren and eight great grandchildren.

When I arrived in Samoa in May 2005, I did not notice any overt racial discrimination or prejudices. The old laws separating the Chinese and the Samoans are, of course, long gone and many people are obviously of mixed blood. Most of the general stores and restaurants are owned by people of Chinese descent, but the lack of anti-Chinese sentiments had made it possible for Chinese, and people of mixed Chinese-Samoan blood, to become civil servants and elected members of parliament. In 1997, the new Miss Pacific was even a Samoan-Chinese, Verona Ah Ching.

Some anti-Chinese feelings have remained though, and, in 2005, an opposition politician, A'eau Peniamina, began to question what he called "China's real motives," and warned Samoans "to be careful of the Chinese [because] they can run you out of business as seen elsewhere." The present Prime Minister, Tuilaepa Sailele Malielegaoi, struck back: "That is racist and I will not stand for any racism in this Parliament." Peniamina's statement was also remarkable in that Taiwan is known to have funded the opposition in Samoa in an attempt to break the country's close relationship with mainland China.

Racism has also surfaced from time and time in neighbouring American Samoa, a small group of islands to the east, which has the official status of being "an unincorporated territory of the United States." Apart from two tuna canneries which export processed fish to the United States, there is not much employment there either, but many American Samoans have joined the US military and are dying in disproportionate numbers in Iraq. When I went there from independent Samoa, I saw yellow ribbons outside houses and on big American cars, which were also bedecked with stickers saying "support our troops."

The people are some of the most obese I have seen, and I found shops well-stocked with tins of corned beef, crates of Coca-Cola and industrial-size jars of mayonnaise. The capital,

Pago Pago, was very dirty and big, aggressive mongrels roamed the streets. It could have been a beautiful place as it girds a dramatic, natural harbour surrounded by green hills. But it is not. Pago Pago is run down and polluted by oil slicks and waste from the tuna canneries.

The New Zealand journalist Michael Field has described American Samoa as "something of a tragedy, a welfare waif with little prospect of ever being taken seriously in the world." Local people seems to exist on government-provided food coupons and other handouts, while the tuna canneries and the related fishing industry have to look to independent Samoa and Korea to hire workers and managers. Next to the Koreans, who are relatively recent arrivals, people of Chinese descent make up the largest Asian community in American Samoa. Many of them have relatives in independent Samoa, but being under American rule, they have closer connections to Hawaii than to their nearest neighbour.

The target for American Samoan racism was not the few Chinese who live there, but the 2,000 Koreans in the fishing business. When Togiola Tulafono was inaugurated as governor of the territory in 2003, a local Christian leader, Siaosi Mageo, caused headlines in the local and American press when he urged the deportation of the Koreans. In the 1980, Mageo said, the Samoans took care of the "African snail problem", an invasion of parasitical snails that devoured all the plants in their way. "Today, we seem to not be able to do anything about the new threat—the Korean snail. One day Samoans would wake up to find they had Korean politicians and a Korean governor. Our people will be reduced to nothing. Wake up Samoa, you are still sleeping. It is shameful, utter shameful, that foreigners come here and rule over us." However, as Michael Field pointed out, "he overlooked the fact that he lived in *American* Samoa."

As the failure of the discriminatory colonial laws in the other Samoa showed, racism has never been a real issue among ordinary inhabitants. The territory is small and the communities live close together. People of different ethnic backgrounds cannot, in the long run, be segregated—which was shown already in the 1930s, when some of the few hundred Germans who had remained in Samoa wanted to show their loyalty to the old motherland by setting up a local Nazi Party. There were pictures of Adolf Hitler in every room in the Concordia Club on Beach Road, where they met, and a large Nazi flag was displayed at the front of the building.

The Nazis in Germany preached racial purity, but the leader of the group in Samoa, Alfred Matthes was a pre-World War I settler—married to a woman from Tonga. Another member was a German with a Jewish wife while other German plantation owners had married Samoans. They had a hard time explaining to their comrades in Germany that their mixed-race children did indeed meet the "Aryan" standards Berlin expected of good Nazis. The German Samoans argued that Polynesian natives should not be considered a "coloured negroid" race but, indeed, an Aryan one. It is unlikely that Berlin accepted this, and in 1939 the Samoan Nazi party was dissolved when Matthes went broke.

I drove around Upolu, the island where Apia is located, but never made it to the larger but less populated island Savaii, which is more traditionally Samoan and Polynesian. Unlike the Melanesians, who are divided into innumerable tribes and sub-tribes speaking different languages, the Polynesians are an ethnically and linguistically relatively cohesive group of people. Similar dialects are spoken inside the triangle formed by Hawaii, New Zealand and Easter Island—which is Polynesia, "the many islands."

Although smaller than Savaii, Upolu is still one of the biggest islands in the region, and it is mountainous, not a coral atoll like many other Pacific islands. And, as on most mountainous Pacific islands, a road follows the coast around Upolu while the interior is virtually uninhabited and covered with tropical rainforests and scrublands. People live scattered around the coast, and I saw hordes of children playing between *fales*, traditional Samoan houses without walls but with wooden posts holding up thatched roofs. There was not much agricultural activity, only a few villagers here and there eking out a living from fishing and small-scale farming, mainly taro, bananas and breadfruit. The main source of income for many families is actually remittances from relatives in New Zealand. There are more than 100,000

Samoans in New Zealand, and the former colonial power has an annual quota of 1,100 Samoans to settle there so more are migrating west every year. There are more Samoans than any other Polynesians in New Zealand except for the native Maoris, and those expatriates support their families back home on the islands.

Few Samoans in their home country seemed to be employed in regular jobs other than for the government, and as waiters in restaurants in Apia, cleaners in hotels and other service jobs. And, typically, when a Chinese firm set up a factory outside Apia to make cashmere garments—a more labour intensive industry—it had to employ women from China for the purpose. Otherwise, there are not many recent Chinese immigrants, perhaps not more than a few hundred. Some of them, I was told, are waiting for Samoan citizenship so they can continue to New Zealand and settle there.

Upolu's main historical attraction is a stately old mansion on a hill overlooking Apia. It was built by the Scottish author Robert Louis Stevenson who settled in Samoa in 1889 and spent the last five years of his life there. He named the mansion "Vailima," or "five waters" in Samoan, after the small streams that run through the property. After his death, it was bought first by a German businessman and then by the German government to serve as the governor's official residence. After 1914, Vailima was where the New Zealand governor resided. When Samoa achieved independence in 1962, it became the official residence of the Heads of State, but now is a museum open to the public.

Samoa is neither a republic nor a hereditary monarchy. Two of Samoa's four paramount chiefs at the time of independence, Tuopua Tamasese Mea'ole and Malietoa Tanumafili II, were appointed joint Heads of State for life. But Tuopua Tamasese Mea'ole died in 1963 leaving Malietoa Tanumafili II as the only Head of State until his death at the age of 94 in June 2007. He was, in effect, a constitutional monarch, but none of his sons succeeded him. Instead, the Parliament elected another chief, Tuiatua Tupua Tamasese Efi, Head of State for a five-year term, thus introducing a more republican form of government. At first, the country was known as "Western Samoa" to distinguish it from American

Samoa, but it is now officially known as "The Independent State of Samoa"—to make an even stronger statement to its non-independent neighbour.

In 1976, a year after Samoa and Beijing established diplomatic relations, Malietoa Tanumafili II traveled to the People's Republic of China on an official state visit, the first by a head of state of a Pacific nation. He was given a red carpet welcome, emphasising the importance Beijing places on relations with the small Pacific states. The Samoan Head of State held talks with the then Chinese Premier Hua Guofeng and, according to an announcement at the time an agreement was signed "on economic and technical cooperation between the two countries," which, in effect, meant Chinese aid to Samoa, as Samoa had nothing offer to China other than its strategic location in the middle of the Pacific Ocean.

Apart from the Government Building in central Apia, China has also provided an interest-free loan to build a women's centre on the outskirts of the capital. In February 2008, China also announced that it would transfer yet another loan on favourable terms, now in the order of 44 million US dollars, to build more government buildings and a conference facility. Since 1976, China has maintained an active embassy in Samoa, the oldest in the Pacific. It is located in a compound near Stevenson's old mansion on the hill south of Apia. And, since 2005, Chinese television has the largest TV presence in the country. Samoa has become China's closest and staunchest ally in the South Pacific.

One reason for China's eagerness to court the Pacific countries is that each state, no matter how small, has a seat at the United Nations. Today, there are twelve independent Pacific nations—excluding New Zealand—and all of them are UN members. Oli Brown, at the Geneva-based International Institute for Sustainable Development, has pointed out that, "in total, the 7.5 million people of the independent states of the Pacific have more voting power in international fora like the General Assembly of the United Nations than the 3.5 billion people of China, India, Japan and the United States combined."

And of those 7.5 million people, more than six million live in Papua New Guinea. The next most populous country is

Fiji with 837,000 inhabitants, followed by the Solomon Islands and 552,000 people. Hence the intense diplomatic rivalry between Taiwan and China. Taiwan wants supporters in the United Nations for diplomatic recognition and its own bid to re-enter the organisation, which it left when Beijing took over China's seat in 1971. China is equally eager to ensure that Taiwan does not get that support, and every vote counts. Tuvalu with 26 square kilometres and Nauru with 21 are the two smallest members by population of the United Nations. Tuvalu has only 11,000 inhabitants and Nauru, the world's smallest republic, 13,000.

But there is also a strategic dimension to China's interest in Polynesia as well as Micronesia, "the small islands." to the northwest. These island nations may lack the mineral resources and forests of Melanesia and they have tiny land areas. But their sea areas and economic exclusion zones are huge. The 100,000 inhabitants of the Republic of Kiribati live on 726 square kilometres of land—but its 32 atolls and one raised coral island are dispersed over 3.5 million square kilometres, a strategically located area in the middle of the Pacific Ocean and straddling the equator. The Kingdom of Tonga has 112,000 inhabitants on 748 square kilometres of land—and an ocean area of 700,000 square kilometres. Even the tiny Cook Islands, still not fully independent but a territory in "free association" with New Zealand, has a sea area of 1.8 million square kilometres. And barely 15,000 Cook Islanders live on 240 square kilometres of land. The outside power that wins over these small island nations can control the Pacific, the world's largest ocean, and the buffer between Asia and America.

One of the most beautiful groups of islands in the Pacific are the Cooks, tiny pearls in a huge ocean and hundreds of kilometres away from the nearest land, French Polynesia in the east and Samoa to the west. The main island, Rarotonga, is mountainous with sharp, scraggy peaks rising to 653 meters above the sea. The next major island, Aitutaki, is a flat atoll made from coral and volcanic rocks and curved around a vast lagoon with crystal clear, turquoise water. The other islands are similar to Rarotonga or Aitutaki, but much smaller. Rarotonga is about the same distance to the south of the Equator as Hawaii is north of it with a similar pleasant tropical climate. Warm, but not steaming hot.

The main town, Avarua, yet another one-street Pacific capital, is perched on the northern shore of Rarotonga. Despite its small size, Avarua is a lively place packed with shops, cafés and galleries. The setting of the town is spectacular with a clear, blue ocean on one side and sharp, green peaks on the other. It is an ideal place for a holiday, but not to live. Seventy-five thousand Cook Islanders, or five times as many as the present population of the islands, have migrated abroad, mostly to New Zealand but also to Australia.

The first European to spot the Cooks was the Spanish explorer Alvaro de Mendana de Neira, who also sailed to the Solomon Islands. He passed the Cooks in 1595, but it was not until the 19th century that they came under foreign domination. The first Christian missionaries arrived in 1823, and with them and European traders came alien diseases which decimated the population to the degree that social structures were unable to function. By 1901 all the islands had been annexed by New Zealand, then a British colony.

No outside cultural force has had more impact on the lives of people in the Pacific than the Christian missionaries. Spanish Jesuits were the first Christians in the region. They came in the 17th century and succeeded in converting the Chamorros of the Marianas and Guam to Catholicism. But this did not happen without bloodshed. At first, the natives resisted the Christian onslaught and many priests and catechists were killed. Spanish troops then burned the villages, and the people were cowed into submission—and nearly all of them became Christians.

The London Missionary Society sent Protestants to Tahiti in 1797, and soon the faith spread to other islands. The American Board of Commissioners for Foreign Missions in Boston sent missionaries to Hawaii in 1819, bringing very strict Puritan ethics to Polynesia. They showed little respect for traditional beliefs and customs and looked on the islanders as barbarian savages who had to be "civilised." Women, who usually went about the islands bare-breasted and with little else covering their bodies than grass-skirts, were given wide, loose-fitting gowns with floral patterns, long sleeves and a high neck. Known as "Mother Hubbard frocks," probably after a female Western missionary, these were intended to cover as much skin as possible and not reveal any curvy, female bodies. Women from New Caledonia to Tahiti still wear that kind of dress, and the only topless females in the region these days are, somewhat ironically, Australian and other Western tourists sunbathing on the beaches.

The missionaries were also aghast at the lax sexual mores of the islanders. If "free love" ever existed, it was on the Pacific islands. Young people mixed freely, and even when married extramarital affairs were not really frowned upon. Ralph Linton wrote in his study of life in the Marquesas Islands, now in French Polynesia: "Young people, from puberty to marriage, formed a group called *kaioi*. From time to time, the *kaioi* would go on tour, performing their dances in the villages of other friendly groups…the *kaioi* dances usually concluded with sexual exhibitions… In addition to this, the girls of the *kaioi* group were expected to entertain visiting males sexually, and they took great pride in the number of men they could satisfy in one evening. Except for taboos in the case of siblings and parents, there was complete sexual licence among these young people."

The dances were not only about sex but also involved worship of traditional gods and spirits, which the missionaries detested. They put an end to most old traditions, which they considered "pagan." Traditional religious paraphernalia were burned or buried and practices such as sensual dancing forbidden. It is only in recent years that Polynesian dance with suggestive hip movement has been revitalised—and now to entertain tourists. Hawaii has become almost synonymous with *hula-hula* and no visit to any Polynesian island is complete without a feast of traditional food—and dancers in grass skirts entertaining and amusing the foreign visitors. The only difference may be that the young women these days are not topless, but have bras made from coconuts. And public copulation, common in the past when dancers performed, is of course a no-no.

The churches became powerful institutions that dominated people's lives. On Sundays, life comes to a standstill all over the Pacific as church bells toll over the islands and people gather to pray and sing hymns. And, in a sense, the accomplishments of the missionaries have not been entirely negative. Many islanders became literate and the missionaries were probably the only white men who did not come to the islands to look for food, profit or women. In Melanesia, the missionaries worked against white blackbirders and put an end to cannibalism and headhunting.

But not many Europeans settled permanently on the islands. The Cooks especially were left more or less alone, and, in August 1965, the territory was proclaimed "a self-governing state in free association with New Zealand." All its inhabitants are citizens of New Zealand with the right of abode there— which is why so many have left—and it uses New Zealand currency. But the Cook Islands has its own government and parliament, and, nowadays, the semi-independent state also runs its own foreign affairs. The association with New Zealand means that it cannot be represented in the United Nations. But the Cook Islands gets millions of dollars in aid from the old colonial power, without which it would not been able to run schools, hospitals and other public services.

In recent years, however, the Cook Islands has developed strong relations with China. The biggest and newest buildings in Avarura are the court house and a police station, both built with Chinese aid and by workers brought in from China. Ron Crocombe, the New Zealand-born dean of Pacific studies and a permanent resident of the Cooks, told me during my visit to the islands that such structures are fairly typical of Chinese aid to the Pacific: China builds symbols of power and authority for the government leaders, and huge sports stadiums for the public at large.

And then there are the "friendship tours." Government officials as well as journalists from the local papers, *Cook Islands News* and the *Cook Islands Times/Herald*, have been invited to China and toured Beijing and other cities. The tours and the aid are Beijing's way of thanking the Cook Islands for, in July 1997, recognising the People's Republic of China and its "One China Policy." In April 2004, a further grant to the Cooks of 4 million New Zealand dollars, or roughly half that amount in US dollars, was announced. Robert Woonton, a former prime minister of the Cooks, was in Beijing at the time and said: "Some people may still be asking what the Chinese will want from us in return for their assistance, but their only requirement is for the Cook Islands to recognise China's legitimate ownership of Taiwan."

That may be the only stated requirement. But China is no doubt also eager to expand its influence over the vast sea area that the Cooks controls, for fishing and, in the long run, to control yet another huge and strategically important piece of the Pacific Ocean. China has offered to build airports and wharfs on the Cooks to facilitate tourism and the fishing industry. But these could also be used for other purposes in times of crises. During World War Two II, the Americans recognised the strategic importance of the Cooks, and built two long runways on Aitutaki, which until 1974 were longer than those at the international airport on Rarotonga. In the 1940s, the Aitutaki airfield played an important role in the Pacific war against Japan, and was used by both the United States and New Zealand militaries.

I met people on the Cooks who felt uneasy with the increasingly closer relationship with China. The Cooks and other Polynesian islands may have a relatively high living standard, higher than Melanesia, but they are tiny, too small and weak to withstand outside pressure—and to reject generous offers of monetary assistance. The Polynesian nations, unlike Melanesia, actually lacks minerals and other natural resources and are heavily dependent on foreign assistance, which makes them less economically independent than, for instance, Papua New Guinea and the Solomon Islands. Aid from China was welcome by the Cook Islanders, but the presence of Chinese construction workers when the courthouse and the police station were built was a major concern. Why not employ local labour?

On September 14, 2004, Zhang Wei, spokesperson for the Chinese embassy in Wellington, New Zealand, wrote in the *Cook Islands News*: "China seeks no self-interest in the South Pacific, non-interference is a fundamental principle underpinning China's relations with South Pacific countries," and, he asserted, "no strings whatsoever" are attached to Chinese aid. The article prompted Ron Crocombe to retort: "All countries' foreign relations contain some self-interest, all influence internal affairs, and all aid has strings (some visible but more hidden—sometimes in the pockets and egos of the powerful.) But in recent years China pursues its self-interests more forcefully, interferes more in Pacific Islands internal affairs, and has more strings attached on its aid than any other country... China's main condition of recognition of any country is that it accepts the 'One China Policy.' That is the public first step. Cook Islanders will have to live with other steps already in progress."

China has also used generosity to try to gain influence in French Polynesia, which actually has the largest of the old Chinese communities in the South Pacific and second in the region only to Hawaii. More than 8,000 people of Chinese descent live there, and the first to settle on Tahiti, the main island, arrived in 1851. But it was not until the great turmoil of 1907-14—when the Emperor was deposed and China became a republic—that large numbers of Chinese came to Tahiti to work on plantations or as labourers in the port and the construction sector.

The opening of a direct steamship line from Hong Kong to Papeete, the capital of French Polynesia, made it easier for Chinese to move in both directions. But fewer left than arrived at Tahiti. Soon, Chinese were running retail stores and other businesses in Tahiti. They also spread to the Tuamoto, Gambier, Marquesas and Austral islands in French Polynesia—and some even went to the Cook Islands. But the number of Chinese who went to the Cooks was small, and almost exclusively male, so many took Polynesian wives. Ron Crocombe believes that probably a quarter of Cook Islanders today have some Chinese ancestry, although they have become almost completely Polynesianised.

The much larger community in French Polynesia was served by a number of associations, and even today there is a building in downtown Papeete with a roof curved in the Chinese style, and "Kuomintang" on a sign outside. Inside, there are portraits of Dr Sun Yat Sen, the founder of the Republic of China, and the flag of the republic which now is confined to Taiwan. The Chinese in French Polynesia have remained loyal to the Nationalists rather than shifting their allegiances to Communist-ruled China. But the rivalry became obvious when the largest Chinese temple in the Pacific was built in Papeete in the late 1980s. Taiwan, or the Republic of China, donated a pair of carved dragons on the pillars as well as carvings and a plaque—while the People's Republic of China's contribution was a pair of stone lions. It was a rare gesture from Beijing to improve its standing among the Chinese of French Polynesia.

The temple also includes a shrine commemorating Chim Soo Kung, a local Chinese martyr, whose fate clearly shows the callousness with which the French once ran their Pacific colonies. During the American Civil War, when shipments of cotton from the southern, Confederate states to England had nearly ceased, William Steward, an Irish adventurer, gained permission from the French—who by the 1840s had seized control of the islands—to establish a cotton plantation on Tahiti. He imported a thousand Chinese on contract, but working conditions were miserable. The demand for cotton from Tahiti also diminished after the Civil War ended in 1865. American exports to Europe picked up again, and the price of Tahitian cotton plummeted. Wages were cut, leading to conflicts between the Chinese workers, Steward and the French authorities.

In 1869, there was a riot among the workers, and one of them was killed and several were injured. Chim Soo Kung accepted the blame, or so the story goes, to save the lives of others who were implicated in the affair. He was strapped down on a guillotine and beheaded. The local Chinese community moved his body to a grand tomb in the Chinese cemetery, where he is still remembered with an annual ceremony on All Saints Day. But nothing remains of the cotton plantation at Atimaono on Tahiti's southern coast, where the riots took place. A golf course now occupies most of the land.

Times have changed and the fact that the Chinese, like the native Polynesians, in French Polynesia are now citizens of France allows them to freely engage in any kind of business and take part in local politics, unlike in countries where the Chinese are considered non-indigenous. French rule also means that immigration, legal and otherwise, is strictly controlled and citizenship cannot be bought. Consequently, there has been no influx of "new" Chinese to

French Polynesia. The "old" Chinese are well established, and some of the richest people in French Polynesia are of Chinese descent. French Polynesia's booming black pearl industry was founded by a second-generation Chinese immigrant, Robert Tan, who also has a partnership with the territory's airline, Air Tahiti Nui. Other Chinese in French Polynesia own shops, ships, road transport, import-export businesses, restaurants and hotels. And they hold their celebrations at the local hall of the Kuomintang.

There is an independence movement in French Polynesia. In fact, its leader, Oscar Temaru, has on three occasions—in 2004, from 2005 to 2006, and from 2007 to 2008—served as president of the partly self-governing territory. But it remains too dependent on French aid to be able to become a fully independent state, and even Temaru has stated that independence has to be achieved gradually. And, despite paying homage to the memory of Chim Soo Kung, most Chinese today remain staunchly pro-French; many fear that their position would be less clear if French Polynesia became independent.

France remains the only Western power besides the United States that still maintains a significant presence in the Pacific. Apart from French Polynesia, New Caledonia in Melanesia and the small Polynesian islands of Wallis and Futuna are also "French Overseas Territories." Britain has given up all its former colonies—except for the island of Pitcairn with only about 50 inhabitants, most of whom are descendants of English and Irish sailors who staged a mutiny on the ship 'Bounty' in 1798, and their Tahitian common-law-wives. New Zealand has given "associate status" to another island territory it used to rule, Niue, and is trying to convince the minute atolls of the Tokelaus—with less than 2,000 inhabitants—to accept the same status. But it was rejected in two UN-sponsored referendums, in February 2006 and October 2007; the Tokelauans seemed happy with being more closely integrated with New Zealand. The local government is also almost entirely dependent on subsidies from New Zealand.

European power in the Pacific is nevertheless waning, and China, although not intending to establish colonies, is expanding its influence on all fronts: economically, politically and diplomatically. A turning point in the fight for control over the Pacific islands came when Tonga in 1998 decided to severe ties with Taiwan, and recognise the People's Republic of China. Until then, Tonga and Taiwan had been very close allies. Tongan ministers were wined and dined in Taipei, and treated as leaders of some bigger and much more important nation. Tonga itself was a sleepy backwater with 170 islands of which 36 are inhabited. Tongatapu, the main island, is a large, flat coral island with lush, tropical vegetation. It is also famous for its flocks of flying foxes and some old structures of coralline stones, some weighing up to 40 tonnes, indicating that the island is the home of an ancient civilisation.

It is not certain how China managed to win over Tonga, but on November 1, 1998, the Taiwanese were suddenly, and for many unexpectedly, told to evacuate the rented building near the waterfront in the capital Nuku'alofa that served as the embassy of the Republic of China. A day later, it was announced that the Kingdom of Tonga and the People's Republic of China had established diplomatic relations. In October 1999, Tongan King Taufa'ahau Tupou IV paid an official visit to China where he received a red-carpet welcome along with promises of aid. And the Chinese were quick to move into Tonga. In July 2000, Wu Quanshu, deputy chief of general staff of China's People's Liberation Army (PLA), visited Tonga, followed in April 2001 by another army deputy, Wei Fulin.

The following month, May 2001, Fu Quanyou, chief of the PLA, held a meeting in Beijing with Tonga's army commander, Tau'aika Uta'atu. Tonga is one of very few Pacific island countries with a military force, and its links with China have grown steadily since the two countries established diplomatic relations. Addressing a New Zealand parliamentary select committee investigating links with Tonga, Kuli Taumoefolau, a former captain in the Tongan army who now lives in New Zealand, warned Australia and New Zealand "to increase their military links with Tonga or risk greater Chinese influence in the Pacific." He said that when he was still in the Tongan army, it was obvious that the Chinese military influence was starting to replace that of Tonga's traditional partners. "They use Tonga as a strategic location for them," Taumoefolau continued. "When I was the acting commanding officer for the training, operations and intelligence unit, I worked closely with two officers from the People's Republic of China, and they were there for martial-arts training, which is good, but you see China is slowly moving up there."

Then, in October 2004, Tongan King Taufa'ahau Tupou IV paid another official visit to China at the invitation of President Hu Jintao. The King passed away in September 2006 at the age of 88, and was succeeded by his eldest son, Siaosi Tupou V—who paid a state visit to China in April 2008. Tupou V has now passed away as well, while on a visit to Hong Kong in March 2012—his body was returned to Tonga for the royal funeral aboard a Chinese chartered aircraft. Evidently, Tonga is important to China, and Beijing spares no effort to maintain friendly relations with the tiny but strategically located Pacific kingdom.

There is no other reason why China would befriend Tonga because it is hard to find a more odd couple: China, atheist and still ruled by the Communist Party—and fundamentalist Christian Tonga where a king wields great political authority over an essentially aristocratic system of government with the country's nobles controlling 70 per cent of the Legislative Assembly.

Christianity permeates every aspect of life in Tonga. I was there on a Sunday, and woke up early in the morning as the church bells began ringing. Stores and restaurants were closed, sports were not allowed and buses and taxis did not run. I met a New Zealander who had been apprehended by the police for mowing his lawn on a Sunday. He was not punished, but told very sternly not to commit such a sacrilege again, on the Holy Day of the week.

While other Polynesian islands are also Christian, Tonga is extreme. And its history is also different from that of other Pacific island nations. It was only under a mild form of British protectorate from 1900 to 1970, never a colony. The kings was allowed to reign over their subjects while Britain looked after defence and foreign affairs. The first missionaries had actually arrived in the 1820s, and they were Wesleyan from Britain and Australia. They managed to put an end to fighting between different clans on the islands and, in 1879, the then king, George Tupou I, appointed a Wesleyan missionary, Shirley Baker, prime minister as well as foreign minister and minister of lands. The king, who was in his 80s, saw his power slip into the hands of Baker, who nevertheless recognised the importance of the monarchy.

In Baker's view, a king had to have a crown like a European monarch. Baker had a crown made in Sydney, Australia, and, at the same time, presented King George with the Great Seal of Tonga and the Royal Standard. The seal, an ornate device containing a cross, a dove, three swords and three stars, bears the motto *Koe otua mo Toga ko Hoku Tofia,* or "God and Tonga are my inheritance." Baker also gave Tonga a national anthem and a legal code to enhance Tonga's status as an independent state. A Royal Palace, now a Nuku-alofa landmark, was built in New Zealand and reassembled in the Tongan capital in 1867. The Victorian-style, wooden building with its rounded tower, oriels and verandahs seems modelled after a colonial residence in a hill station established by the British in India.

But Baker's activities were regarded by other Europeans as ridiculous and something of a comic opera. Some Tongans also resented him as he had set up a new church, the "Free Church of Tonga." Some of the natives, however, were loyal to their original Wesleyan church and infighting erupted on the islands. Baker narrowly escaped an assassination attempt in 1887, but his son and daughter were both wounded. Six Tongans were executed for this attack on Baker, and many were deported to other islands. In 1890 Sir John Bates Thurston, a British colonial officer in Fiji, visited Tonga and deported the maverick Baker to Auckland, New Zealand, for being "prejudicial to the peace and good order of the Western Pacific."

The legal code that Baker introduced laid the groundwork for Tonga's strict, Christian-inspired laws. For instance, fornication and adultery were made criminal offences and punishable by hefty fines. This prompted Alfred Maudsley, the British vice consul in Tonga, to say in 1879: "The laws dealing with the relations of the sexes have more the appearance of a missionary wishing to punish sin than a statesman wishing to prevent the increase of crime."

Baker paid a short visit to Tonga in 1897 and returned for good in 1900. In May of that year, Britain and Tonga had signed a treaty placing the islands under British protection—presumably from people like Baker and other outside threats to the sovereignty and integrity of the kingdom. Baker lived the last years of his life peacefully, and without power. He died in Tonga in November 1903, and his grave on the island of Ha'apai is now a tourist attraction. And his legacy still lingers in daily life, the dominant role of the Church and the strength of the monarchy.

Tonga's special status before 1970s meant that few outsiders apart from missionaries settled there. Unlike other islands, where outside men have mixed with local women, the Tongans have remained "pure" Polynesians and Tongan society is astonishingly traditional. Since independence, however, more missionaries have come, many of them from the Latter-day Saints, better known as the Mormons, who have had remarkable success in Tonga. Mormon temples and schools can be seen all over the islands, well-kept houses with manicured lawns. The rate of conversion to Mormonism can perhaps be explained most easily with the benefits that come with membership in The Church of Jesus Christ of Latter-day Saints. Free and advanced education is only one benefit of church membership; it is also known to pay people's electricity bills and other utilities, and many Tongans have been granted scholarships to study in Salt Lake City, Utah, the original home of the Mormons.

However, the Mormons and other missionaries did not upset traditional economic patterns as much as Chinese migrants did when they began to arrive in Tonga in the 1980s. Before that, there was not a single Chinese-owned grocery store in the country. By the early 2000s, more than 70 per cent of all stores were owned by newly-arrived Chinese migrants, who made up 3,000-4,000 of Tonga's population of 100,000. In 2001, Tonga began to expel hundreds of Chinese who had become victims of a wave of ethnic violence. In that year, there had been about 100 cases of assault, armed robbery, burglary and arson of Chinese-owned shops carried out by native Tongans.

The Chinese embassy in Nuku'alofa expressed concern about the level of violence against its nationals while the chief immigration officer, Susana Fotu, said the expulsions were in response to "widespread anger at the growing presence of the storekeepers" and the fear that the Chinese had come to dominate the economy. The main source of income for native Tongans were remittances from relatives abroad, mainly in New Zealand. In Tonga, there were few employment opportunities for ordinary people, and all the stores had been taken over by hard-working Chinese with whom local storeowners had found it impossible to compete. It was a clash between two cultures: Tongan storekeepers were laid-back and relaxed, and their stores served more as meeting places for local men than commercial outlets; the Chinese had come to make money, and kept their stores open all day and night, except, of course, on Sundays when they had to be closed. The Chinese were also able to bring in Chinese consumer goods, which were much cheaper than New Zealand and Australian ones sold by Tongan storekeepers, who were soon put out of business.

The expulsions did not put an end to the violence. When I visited Nuku'alofa in June 2005, a young woman was among many Tongans who told me that the locals deeply resented the influx of Chinese migrants. And, she said, it was not uncommon that young Tongan men robbed Chinese-run stores and beat up the owners. A youth gang would get together, decide which store to attack on a certain day, and then rob it. Or they would stop cars driven by Chinese, beat them and rob them. "The police always arrive too late, and there are never any witnesses to the attacks," the Tongan lady told me.

A year and a half later, in November 2006, years of simmering discontent reached a breaking point. Ostensibly demonstrating for democratic reforms, angry mobs looted and burned at least 30 Chinese-owned stores. Cars were overturned and a reporter from the local news agency, *Tonga News*, described the looting: "Nuku'alofa is an inferno. Shoreline headquarters is gone, the Leiola Duty Free Store, Pacifica Royal Hotel, and major Chinese outlets are up in smoke. Chinese stores were smashed and empty, save for mobs to carry booty of everything from toilet paper to boxes of chicken."

The mayhem did not end until Australian and New Zealand peacekeepers arrived, as they had done in the Solomon Islands a few months earlier. The Tongan army and police enforced martial law is some areas of Tongatapu where Nuku'alofa is located. The official Chinese news agency *Xinhua* reported that the embassy in Nuku'alofa was trying to contact all Chinese residents to make sure they were safe. And, as was the case in the Solomons, Australia could, by intervening militarily, show the rest of the region that it was still a power to be reckoned with, regardless of increased China's influence in Tonga and elsewhere in the Pacific.

At the forefront of the riots were local youth gangs, unemployed and angry young men. Seven of them were killed, caught by a fire they had set at the royal-owned offices of the electricity supplier Shoreline. And around 1,000 were arrested when the riots were suppressed. Most of them belonged to a group calling themselves the Tongan Crip Gang—and they were Mormons. When young Tongans were sent to Salt Lake City for further education, they never fitted in. They began to organise youth gangs in the Mormon capital, only to be deported back to Tonga if they had committed crimes. Joined by young Tongans who had returned from New Zealand, they became a powerful force—and they were the ones who destroyed Nuku'alofa in 2006. The Chinese became an easy target as they were despised by large segments of the population.

It is unlikely that the Tongan authorities will be able to prevent similar riots in the future, and Tonga may well be a testing case for the Chinese authorities preparedness to intervene if the lives of their citizens are in danger. And it is important for Beijing to maintain its influence over this island nation with its vast ocean area.

China has also made considerable inroads in Fiji, where they are rapidly replacing the old Asian community in that island nation: Indians, who were brought in as indentured labour by the British colonial power in the late 19th and early 20th century. Most of them came from Bengal and Bihar and worked in sugar plantations—and brought with them Indian culture, religion and social structures to the South Pacific. Fiji's capital Suva, where many of them, now live, is the largest and most cosmopolitan city in the Pacific after Honolulu. It is well-planned with old colonial buildings between modern structures, green parks and a pleasant botanical garden. The hotels are some of the best in the Pacific, and it is probably the only place in the region where authentic Indian curries are served in small food shops. The native Fijians, who make up just over half the population, are considered Melanesians because of their dark complexion and frizzy hair, but most of their historical and cultural contacts have been with the Polynesian groups of Tonga and Samoa.

Unlike Fijians, who mostly live in villages along the coast of the islands, most Indians are concentrated in the sugar cane-growing areas and live in isolated farm houses, or in towns. Driving across the main island of Viti Levu, one can see shops with signboards in Hindustani, the main language spoken by the Fijian Indians, and small dairy farms with cows for milk production. There are also Hindu temples in the towns as well as the countryside, and even some mosques, which gives Fiji a different feel from other Pacific islands. The caste system has been retained among the Hindu Indians, while the Muslims stick to their beliefs, which means that women are subordinate to men.

The Indians may have come as labourers, and many of them still are, but like the Chinese elsewhere in the Pacific, they soon came to dominate trade and commerce in Fiji, and soon even politics. At the 1986 census, 46 per cent of the country's 715,537 inhabitants were Fijian—and outnumbered by 48.7 per cent Indians. Fiji became independent in 1970 after 96 years of British rule, and as long as the colonial power was there, ethnic tensions were kept under wraps. But then, in 1975, racial harmony was jolted as Sakiasi Butadroka, leader of the newly formed Fijian National Party, proposed in parliament that the entire Indian population of Fiji should be repatriated to India. The Indians responded by rallying behind the local Labour Party, which was set up in 1986. It allied itself with the Federation Party, and the coalition won the election in April

1987. But the new government was short-lived; four weeks later, the army staged a coup and a military government led by Lieutenant-Colonel Sitiveni Rabuka seized power. He staged a second coup in September that year, assuming for himself and the army wide-ranging powers including rigid media censorship. On October 7, Rabuka declared Fiji a republic; until then, the British Queen had been the head of state, as she is in Australia, New Zealand and some other former British colonies. Indian homes were attacked by mobs of ultranationalist Fijians with the army and the police egging them on.

Australia and New Zealand condemned the coups and suspended aid. India was also forthright in its criticism—and diplomatic relations between Fiji and India were severed. The coup led to the departure of many Indian businessmen and shopkeepers to Australia, New Zealand and Canada. Many of Fiji's old Chinese residents also left. They—and the Indians—were, however, replaced by new migrants from China. No exact figure has been mentioned, but the number of migrants is significant, and growing. Estimates vary between 5,000 and 22,000. Fiji's authorities privately put the number at about 15,000, but, as Robert Keith-Reid, editor of *Islands Business* until his death in May 2006, told me when I was in Suva in 2005: "The government doesn't want to mention the actual figure publicly because of fear of a backlash."

A stroll along Victoria Parade, Suva's main thoroughfare, reveals as many shop signs in Chinese as in English, and considerably more than in Hindustani, in front of restaurants, travel agents, bars, private karaoke clubs and general stores. And not all Chinese migrants are law-abiding businesspeople. In Suva, I met Andrew Hughes, an Australian who had been called in to serve as Commissioner of Police because of internal problems in the force. He was adamant that Chinese criminal gangs had established themselves in Fiji and that they were engaged in prostitution, gambling, drugs, passport fraud, corruption in the fisheries' industry and corrupting local officials. In November 2000, 357 kilogrammes of heroin was seized in Fiji, not for local consumption but to be smuggled on to Australia and North America. The heroin came from Southeast Asia's Golden Triangle, and the gangs thought that Fiji would be a convenient trans-shipment point for drugs destined for world markets. Who would suspect that a container arriving from Fiji would contain Southeast Asian heroin?

This has caused concern among Fiji's old-time Chinese population. Bessie Ng Kumlin Ali, a Fijian-Chinese, wrote in her very personal book *The Chinese in Fiji* about a 1996 government scheme to invite Chinese from Hong Kong to settle in Fiji after the 1997 handover to China: "Leaders of the Chinese community themselves have voiced their reservation about an influx, which had the potential to spoil long-established, hard-won relations with other communities. Police commissioner Hughes confirmed those fears when I interviewed him in Suva's central police station: "Old-timers are worried. Especially about the influx of shady newcomers."

The first Chinese to arrive in Fiji were cooks and carpenters on American and Australian ships that had come to pick up sandalwood for the market in Guangzhou in the early 19th century. They were followed by two waves of traders, who set up stores on the islands in the 1850s and 1870s. As in Samoa, many were from the Taishan area in Guangdong province. When gold was discovered on Viti Levu in 1868, more Chinese arrived, but from Melbourne in Australia. They later found a niche in carpentry, cooking, retail, vegetable gardening and other service trades. They were never nearly as numerous as the Indians, and at no stage before the recent influx were there more than 5,000 Chinese in Fiji. But, after generations of hard work, most of them had become relatively wealthy, and loyal to the Nationalist Chinese Kuomintang, which even had an office in an old colonial mansion in Suva that doubled as a consulate for the Republic of China.

When Britain established diplomatic relations with Beijing in 1951, the consulate was closed and its staff returned to Taiwan. Independent Fiji recognised the People's Republic of China in 1975, and, given the sentiments of many local Chinese is almost paranoid about blocking Taiwan from establishing closer links with the islands. Fiji has not recognised Taiwan, but there is in Suva a "trade mission," Taiwan's usual name for its unofficial diplomatic offices overseas. Fiji, in turn, has encouraged investment from both China and Taiwan to make up for the loss of Indian-run businesses and aid from Western democracies. But it is definitely closer to Beijing than to Taipei.

The Chinese community is acutely aware of this and now maintains a cautious balance between China and Taiwan. The national days of the People's Republic—October 1—as well as that of the Republic—October 10—are celebrated with public events sponsored by the respective representatives in Suva. Fiji's Chinese school, named after the first provisional president of the Chinese Republic, Sun Yat Sen, benefits from a supply of teachers from Taiwan as well as the mainland. The primary school teachers come from Taiwan and the secondary from China.

In July 2007, a Fiji/China Business Council was set up, and the inauguration ceremony was attended by the Chinese *chargé d'affaires* in Suva. The guest of honour was Commodore Josaia Voreqe "Frank" Bainimarama, the country's new military leader, who had seized power in yet another coup in December 2006. Aid from Western countries had been cut again after that coup, so Bainimarama made a plea to China: "The Interim Government is also actively pursuing enhanced level of developmental collaboration with China. In particular, we are working on a number of proposals to seek developmental and soft loan funding from China to assist with upgrading of our rural roads and maritime transportation, provide low cost housing to squatters, improve our water supply and revitalise Fiji's agricultural sector. I am determined to ensure that Fiji is able to secure the much needed assistance within this year to provide the services, infrastructure and facilities I have just mentioned for the benefit of ordinary people of this country." He also pledged to relax visa requirements for Chinese nationals, "to encourage tourism."

Chinese aid to Fiji has skyrocketed since the last coup in December 2006, from 900,000 to 135 million US dollars. A May 2008 article in the *Sydney Morning Herald* stated that, "Just as Australia and other Western donors are trying to squeeze [Fiji's] rebel Government, China has dramatically stepped up its aid, effectively dissipating any pressure Western donors might have been generating." The author of the article suggested that China did not wish to risk antagonising Fiji and thus unwittingly push the Bainimarama government towards seeking aid from Taiwan: "China clearly finds itself boxed into a corner. On the one hand, Western states are asking it to help isolate the new dictatorship in Fiji. On the other, China faces the risk of losing a Fiji starved of funds to its renegade province, Taiwan."

In August 2008, Bainimarama visited Beijing, where he stated: "Fiji will not forget that, when other countries were quick to condemn us following the events of 1987, 2000 and 2006, China and other friends in Asia demonstrated a more understanding and sensitive approach to events in Fiji. The Government of the People's Republic of China expressed confidence in our ability to resolve our problems in our way, without undue pressure or interference." The year of the first coup was 1987; in 2000 there were other upheavals as a group of renegade soldiers led by a man called George Speight took the entire cabinet hostage, including Mahendra Pal Chaudhry, who in 1999 had become Fiji's first prime minister of Indian origin. These events led to a military intervention in politics. And 2006, of course, referred to Bainimarama's own seizure of power. On another visit to Beijing, in August 2010, Bainimarama stated that the Chinese understand the "reforms" he is trying to implement "better than Australia and New Zealand do." The Fijian strongman also said that he would "direct diplomatic efforts toward Beijing in the hope of more donations and trade opportunities."

When Western countries make "unreasonable" demands for democracy and good governance, China is always willing to step in, in Fiji as in Papua New Guinea. China is indeed here to stay, anti-Chinese riots or no riots in Tonga and the Solomon Islands.

CHAPTER FOUR
THE THIRD WAVE

The coastline of China's southern Fujian province is one of the most rugged in the country. Only 512 kilometres from one end to the other as the crow flies, it zig-zags in and out along 3,752 kilometres of actual coast with more than 1,000 offshore islands. A few of these still belong to the Republic of China and serve as proof that it is, indeed, more than just "the province of Taiwan." Jinmen, or Quemoy in the local dialect, is only about a kilometre from the island of Xiamen, or Amoy, in the People's Republic of China. Here, Nationalist and Communist China stand eyeball-to-eyeball in one of the last outposts of the Cold War. The Matsu islands further to the north are also part of "Fujian Province, the Republic of China," and rise from the sea not far from the provincial capital and port city of Fuzhou.

Fujian's interior is mountainous and the province is traditionally described as "eight parts mountain, one part water, and one part farmland." Most people live along the coast and it is from here that millions of people over the centuries have gone to seek greener pastures abroad, in Southeast Asia, the Pacific and North America. But they did not run away from poverty, as the stereotypical explanation has it. A Fujianese friend of mine points out that the province is actually one of the most prosperous in China—but it has a long tradition of seafaring and migration. He described the Fujianese as a "footloose people" who traditionally have been focused on the sea and what may be beyond it. Also, Fujian has always been a volatile frontier area, which explains its near-permanent state of flux. During the first two major waves of migration—after the fall of the Ming dynasty in the

17th century and the upheavals of the mid-19th century—most of the people who left China came from Fujian. Until the recent wave of migration, 80 per cent of the Chinese in the Philippines, 55 per cent in Indonesia, 50 per cent in Burma, and 40 per cent in Singapore were of Fujian origin.

But in the past, migration was still quite localised. The vast majority of migrants left from three counties near Fuzhou, but seldom from the provincial capital itself. For generations, able-bodied men—and some women as well—from Lianjiang, Minhou and Changle have gone overseas to toil as labourers. They have sent money home to enable their families to build houses and have a reasonably good life. This culture of migration, rather than poverty, has been the push-factor. The pull-factor for those staying behind is that some day one of their sons or daughters will join their even more prosperous relatives in North America, Australia or Southeast Asia. From the Fuqing area in the south, people have gone to Japan, while natives of Pingtan islands head for Taiwan, all on boats owned and operated for the most part by Taiwanese smugglers. The local Chinese dialect in all those areas is close to the language spoken on Taiwan, and, with ethnic affinity bridging the political divide, links across the strait have always been strong.

An old Fujianese saying goes: "Plant a tree in America—rest in the shade in China." The situation in parts of Guangdong province to the south is somewhat similar. Taishan, or Toishan in the local dialect, has supplied North America in particular—and parts of the Pacific—with more labourers than any other part of Guangdong and even all China. The first were recruited in the 1870s to replace slave labour in the United States, and these were followed by more migrants who made it to New York and other American cities, and to Toronto in Canada. The discovery of gold in California provided further stimulus for Chinese to emigrate to the United States.

Until the late 1980s, people of Taishan ancestry—or from the neighbouring districts of Kaiping, Xinhiui and Enping, also in the district of Siyi—accounted for 70 per cent of all Chinese Americans. After the Fujianese, the Cantonese were the most numerous of migrants in the past. However, because of official segregation policies, the Chinese immigrants had to stay in parts of the towns and cities where no one else wanted to live. Based on this exclusion, the well-known Chinatowns developed not only in the United States but in many other Western countries as well.

Chinese from Shantou, also in Guangdong province, migrated primarily to Thailand, but to other parts of Southeast Asia and the United States as well. In Pinyin, or standardised Mandarin Chinese, they are called *Chaozhou* while they are known as Chiu Chow in the United States and Hong Kong. In Thailand, they are called Teochew, and the vast majority of Sino-Thais come from the Shantou area, which they call "Swatow." They began to arrive in Bangkok on British steamships in the early and mid-19th century, and the community went through the usual transition from labourers and coolies to merchants, business tycoons and bankers. And for generations they have been sending money back to their families in and around Shantou. It is not unusual to see signs in both Chinese characters and the Thai alphabet outside shops in Shantou.

But now, in the era of the third wave of migration, people have moved overseas from many other parts of China as well, and they are migrating to parts of the world where few if any went in the past. Hungary has received the largest influx of Chinese in Eastern Europe. Most of them come from the provinces bordering the Russian Far East who have caught the Trans-Siberian Express to Moscow and then travelled on to Budapest. Many of these Chinese are ethnic Koreans, and they now control several huge markets in Budapest where they began by selling consumer goods brought with them on the train from China. Nowadays there are thousands of shops, restaurants, and even plazas run by Chinese in Hungary. In 2007, textile factories in Romania employed hundreds of workers from China to get around the country's chronic labour shortages. Ethnic Koreans from China—along with Mongolians—have settled in South Korea, which until recently had very few foreign workers. Chinese migration to the Russian Far East is also an entirely new phenomenon.

Japan has received migrants from Shandong as well as Shanghai and Beijing. Many of them are students who have overstayed and found jobs in services and the entertainment industry. Yunnanese, some of them belonging to the Hui Muslim minority, have joined distant relatives in northern Thailand, bolstering Chinese-Muslim communities which have been there since the mid-19th century. Yunnanese have also moved into northern Burma and Laos. Chinese from all over have settled in Cambodia. And Chinese communities in North America are no longer dominated by people of Taishan descent; newly-arrived Fujianese now make up a majority in New York's fabled Chinatown, but have also settled elsewhere in the United States and Canada. Chinese businesses—import-export agencies, travel bureaus and money-changers—are evident in Dubai in the United Arab Emirates.

In February 2004, 18 cockle pickers—all of them illegal immigrants from China—died after becoming trapped by rising tides in Lancashire's Morecambe Bay in Britain. Until then, few were aware of the presence of Chinese cockle pickers in the country. In an even more tragic incident in 2000, 58 Chinese illegal immigrants perished inside the cargo hold of a truck whose only air vent was closed. Only two people survived.

Some adventurous Chinese from a variety of provinces have migrated as far as South Africa, Nigeria and Angola, where they now run stores and small businesses. Africa, with its rich mineral resources, has also become important as a source of raw materials. In Zambia, Chinese work in copper and coal mining and China is also pouring in thousands of its own blue collar workers to manage its enterprises—which has caused resentment in a country with some 80 per cent unemployment. The fact that Chinese workers are kept in dormitory-style housing on the outskirts of town with little contact with the local people only adds to suspicion and prejudice.

A strong pull factor, which in some ways marked the beginning of the third wave of Chinese migration, was the United States' decision in December 1978 to shift recognition from the Republic of China to the People's Republic. China then liberalised its previously strict emigration regulations in order to qualify for most-favoured status with the United States. Since 1979, tens of thousands of Chinese have legally emigrated to the United States and other countries. But, as Chin Ko-lin, an American scholar who was born into the Fujianese community in Burma, has pointed out: "US immigration quotas allow only a limited number of Chinese whose family members are US citizens or who are highly educated to immigrate to or visit America, Beginning in the late 1980s, some of those who did not have legitimate channels to immigrate began turning to human smugglers for help." Chin says that immigration officials in Taiwan, Hong Kong, Macau, Japan, Australia, Hungary, Romania, Italy, Spain, the Netherlands and Canada are also alarmed by the dramatic increase in the number of "undocumented Chinese" arriving in these countries and territories.

In the 1980s and early 1990s, many Chinese migrants undertook risky journeys hidden in the hulls of dilapidated ships and freighters. In the most famous case, on June 6, 1993, a rickety, 30-metre freighter called the *Golden Venture*, ran aground at Rockaway Point in Queen's, New York. The *Golden Venture* was not a big vessel, but nearly 300 people, all of them from Fujian, emerged from its cargo hold. Some 200 of them threw themselves into the cold waters in the hope of reaching the shore. Many could not swim and ten of them drowned.

The ship had sailed from Thailand via Singapore, Mombasa in Kenya and the small port of Infanta in South Africa, and then across the Atlantic to the United States. Originally, there were only 100 migrants onboard the *Golden Venture*, but 200 more were picked up in Mombasa because their ship had broken down. There was almost a mutiny onboard when the ship was going to pick up even more Chinese waiting at Infanta—but the "passengers" were kept in check by armed enforcers from the gang they had paid to be smuggled to America.

It had taken four months for the *Golden Venture* to reach New York, where its dramatic arrival became headline news. Newspapers were filled with reports of people smuggling rings and TV networks carried the dramatic footage of illegal immigrants as, shivering and huddling under blankets, they were rescued from the waves and led away by the police. That this was taking place less than an hour's voyage from

73

the Statue of Liberty made the drama even more emotional and divided the United States between those who thought the poor and oppressed should be welcomed as heroes in the 'Land of the Free', and others who saw the massive illegal immigration as a threat to national security. And who were the so-called "snakeheads"—the men with tattoos, pistols and knives? And what kind of worldwide network did they belong to, as they had contacts in widely disparate countries such as Thailand, Kenya and South Africa?

After the arrival of the *Golden Venture* and the publicity and controversy the saga generated, the smugglers became more discreet and their methods more sophisticated. According to a United States intelligence report that was compiled a year later, in June 1994, Chinese smuggling organisations had "vastly expanded their elaborate networks of way stations around the world and [were] now capable of transporting tens of thousands of people into the United States." According to the report, one of the most roundabout air routes originated in Bangkok, whence migrants would travel by air to New Delhi and Karachi, then to Nairobi or Johannesburg, and then to Buenos Aires or Rio de Janeiro. Finally, they would fly from Buenos Aires or Rio de Janeiro to either Madrid, Barcelona or London, and finally to New York City. Others have tried to go via even more unexpected routes. In November 1997, the Danish immigration authorities in Greenland detained 21 Chinese trying to enter on false Japanese passports. They had hoped to continue from the huge and sparsely populated, icy island near the North Pole to Canada or the United States.

Regardless of the route, the first stopover is usually Bangkok. Any Chinese national can get a visa-on-arrival stamped into their passports for a 30-day tourism stay in Thailand. There, they obtain doctored or false Singaporean or Japanese passports. Fake travel documents of any kind are easily obtained in Bangkok—albeit for a steep price—at several shops in the city's gritty Lad Phrao district, a regional hub for forging passports and visas.

The migrants then leave Thailand on their legitimate Chinese passports. A common destination after Bangkok is Tokyo's Narita airport. They have usually bought a round-trip ticket from Beijing or Shanghai to Bangkok with an airline that has a layover in Tokyo on the return journey. So they check in at Bangkok's airport for their return flight, but in the transit lounge at Narita, they will be met by a member of a trafficking gang who will hand them boarding passes for a flight to the United States with the same, or similar, name as in the false Japanese or Singaporean passports they have obtained in Bangkok. These do not have to have a visa for the United States stamped in them as Singaporeans and Japanese can take advantage of the visa waiver programme when they arrive in Los Angeles, San Francisco or Honolulu. The gang member has checked in at Tokyo with another fake passport with the same name on a flight to the United States, and another flight as well for himself, using his real passport when passing through immigration. In that way, he ends up having two boarding passes, one for the migrant and another for himself.

The false passports may not be good enough to fool immigration officials at airports. But they are meant to show airline employees who only check whether the name on the passport matches that on the ticket when a passenger checks in and actually boards the plane. The Chinese migrant has then discarded his own, real Chinese passport and gets on the plane. Up in the air, the migrant tosses his false passport and the boarding pass in the airplane toilet and then applies for political asylum on landing in the United States, or in Europe, if that is the destination. All applications for political asylum must be considered by Western courts, and carrying a false passport supplied by human trafficking gangs seldom helps migrants win their cases. On the final leg of the journey, all documentation therefore must be destroyed to make it impossible for immigration officials to retrace the migrant's journey, which could lead to forced repatriation.

The smuggling packages sold by the gangs to migrants and others usually include false or real passports, air tickets and sometimes escorts who make sure the migrants safely reach their destinations. The going rate for a one-way passage to the United States is around 35,000-40,000 US dollars. An "informal ticket" from China to Europe, a less popular destination, is much cheaper at only 10,000-15,000 US dollars.

It is also possible to sneak into the United States through the backdoors of its outlying territories. One particularly popular destination is the Commonwealth of the Northern Mariana Islands in the Pacific, which is a US territory but with its own visa waiver programme that includes Chinese citizens. That has enabled many Chinese migrants to work in garment factories and other enterprises on the main island of Saipan, or visit the casino on the nearby island of Tinian, which is rumoured by local residents to be owned by interests close to the Chinese People's Liberation Army. The Northern Marianas and American Samoa are the only US territories that have their own immigration rules. But American Samoa is too difficult and expensive to get to, so it is the Commonwealth of the Northern Marianas that has become a stepping-stone on the way to United States proper. In April 2003, China Southern Airlines began direct flights from Shanghai to Saipan, and the number of Chinese visitors soared.

A visit pass for the Northern Marianas, however, does not entitle the holder to travel on to any other US territories—but Guam, another US territory, is only a couple of hours away by boat. And Guam is inside the US customs and immigration area, and an application for asylum there is usually transferred to the US mainland. Thus, the chance of being sent back to China is minimal.

The illegal migrants are also instructed what to say when applying for asylum in the Western countries of their choice. This has made it much more difficult to determine who is a genuine refugee and who is taking advantage of the 1951 Refugee Convention, which Western countries adhere to. But that does not mean that they are always able to pass the test. An American immigration official told me that he once interviewed an asylum seeker from China who claimed to be a Christian and thus feared for his life if he was sent back to China. When the officer asked him how Jesus died, the asylum seeker replied: "The communists shot him with a machine-gun."

Many others have claimed to be members of the banned Falun Gong movement—but failed when asked to demonstrate how they practice *xigong's* meditative pose. Still others have maintained that they are homosexuals, an illegal orientation in China, even while their travel companion girlfriends wait for them outside the interview room. But most Chinese are granted admission, assisted by a growing number of US lawyers in New York and other major American cities who specialise in helping asylum seekers and know the loopholes in the law.

Because of the growing number of immigrants who have abused the asylum system, those who are legitimately seeking sanctuary abroad from political oppression at home are finding it harder to get accepted—and that applies not only to refugees from China. But human smuggling, especially but not exclusively of Chinese migrants, is now a multi-billion dollar business. And the business will only grow as long as the chances of successful migration to the West are so high and the penalties for getting caught so low. Regulated migration between various countries is a normal, global phenomenon and but the illegal nature of a large portion of Chinese migration not only to the West but also to other parts of Asia and the South Pacific is also bound to result in social problems in those countries as it involves criminal gangs. Illegal migration breeds corruption within the law enforcement authorities there as well. As we have seen, this problem is especially serious in the chaotic Russian Far East, and the small and therefore vulnerable nations of the South Pacific.

Chin Ko-lin, one of the world's foremost experts on human smuggling and Chinatown gangs, points out that this lucrative business is run by many groups, both small and large, working independently—each with its own organisation, connections, methods and routes or, in short, its own worldwide web of contacts and actors. The main players, or the "big snakeheads" as Chin calls them, are generally Chinese living overseas who invest money in a smuggling operation and oversee it, but they are usually not known by those being smuggled. Or, if they are based in China, they are either former or current Chinese government employees.

Then there are "small snakeheads," who are hired by the big ones to guide and move the illegal immigrants, to charter boats or arrange air tickets, and to act as enforcers during the journey to the United States. Other "small snakeheads" down the line include support personnel who provide food and lodging to illegal immigrants at transit points on the way and, worst of all, the debt collectors. These are thugs who collect smuggling fees in advance from the migrants or their families—and lock up those who have not paid in the so-called "safe houses" until their debt is settled. The "small snakeheads" receive all the media attention because of the sensational aspects associated with their "duties" along the line—but the "big snakeheads" who hired them can always find new ones. Enforcers are easily replaceable and the smashing of one gang does not in any way affect the overall people smuggling business as only the "small snakeheads" get caught.

And then there is the general attitude to the traffic in China itself. Many people Chin met in, for instance, Fujian, thought of snakeheads as "philanthropists" and appreciated their services. A 43-year-old male from Tingjiang in Fujian told Chin: "I look at human smuggling as benevolent work because a snakehead can help people out of their predicament." A 19-year-old woman described the snakeheads as "good people because, in a way, they help China solve her overpopulation problem." Even a government official admitted: "Frankly, we have an ambivalent attitude towards illegal migration. On the one hand, we hope our villagers will have an opportunity to go abroad and make money, because this will solve our high unemployment rate. Also, money sent back by migrants helps us to construct the local infrastructure. On the other hand, since migration without proper documents is against our law, we must carry out the orders from above and stop illegal migration. Consequently, when it comes to dealing with illegal migration, we usually keep one eye open and close the other."

While travelling to their final destinations, some migrants do not have to use false passports, and it is not only genuine Papua New Guinea ones that can be bought. The first country to develop a "passport of convenience" scheme was Tonga. The idea came in the early 1980s from a Hong Kong-based American investment adviser and former Bank of America employee, Jesse Bogdanoff. He had also once had a company that sold magnets to cure back pain. Of all people, Bogdanoff was asked by King Taufa'ahau Tupou IV for advice on how to raise badly needed revenue. The banker-and-magnet-salesman's suggestion was to sell passports. Britain had then just signed an agreement with China for the return of Hong Kong, and a new category of British passports had been introduced for most residents of the territory. They were "overseas dependents," which meant that they had no right of abode in Britain, and the new passports were of dubious value even as ordinary travel documents.

For 10,000 US dollars, anyone could become a "Tongan Protected Person" and carry a special Tongan passport. As the bearers still required visas to enter Tonga, many countries, among them Australia and New Zealand, refused to recognise these passports. So in 1984 a new law was passed allowing ordinary Tongan passports and naturalisation certificates to be issued to anyone willing to pay 20,000 US dollars. Now, there were many takers, and not all of them were Hong Kong Chinese. Among the first who became Tongans were ex-President Ferdinand Marcos of the Philippines and his wife Imelda, after a popular uprising in 1986 had forced them to flee their country. Then came Chinese settlers, who took over much of the commerce on the islands—which eventually led to the November 2006 riots in Nuku'alofa.

Tonga shut down the practice in late 1998 and made the fateful decision to place the profits from the sale of passports—an estimated 24.5 million US dollars—with a company in Nevada called Millennium Asset Management. Bogdanoff even persuaded the king to appoint him as the official court jester—just to get the last laugh and disappear with most of the money. It turned out that Millennium Asset Management had been set up for the sole purpose of receiving the money from Tonga, and then ceased to exist. In the end, Tonga gained nothing from its unorthodox passport scheme. Dave Barry, a *Washington Post* columnist, asked wryly how a country could have gone wrong "with a financial adviser who is both a court jester and a seller of health magnets."

But Tonga's bitter experiences from selling passports have not deterred the Republic of Kiribati, the Marshall Islands, Nauru, Tuvalu and Vanuatu from following suit. For a fee, it has at times been possible to obtain a passport from any of those Pacific island nations. The Marshall Islands, a former US territory, became self-governing in 1986 and fully independent in 1991. It first established diplomatic relations with China, and through its mission in Beijing began to sell passports for 25,000 to 40,000 US dollars apiece. Most of the estimated 2,000 Marshallese passports were sold during 1995-1996 and the sale had an enormous appeal since all Marshallese citizens were allowed free access to live and work in the United States in accordance with an agreement reached when the islands became independent.

The United States government began to exert pressure on the Marshalls to stop the practice and it was supposed to have ended in 1997. But according to Giff Johnson of the *Marshall Islands Journal*, who I met during my visit to the islands, predated passports continued to be sold. Then, in 1998, the Marshall Islands suddenly announced a major shift in foreign policy and formally recognised the Republic of China, which now maintains an embassy in Majuro. The deal came with promises of generous aid from Taipei, so the sale of passports was longer necessary to fill the coffers in the resource-starved country of some 50,000 people.

It was stopped, but the passport scheme nevertheless put the Marshall Islands on the map of many Chinese. Some actually settled in the tiny capital of Majuro, a 56-kilometre long and only a few hundred metres wide coral atoll where the highest point is an arched bridge between two of the islets in the chain. There may not be more than 500 Chinese in Majuro, but their impact has been tremendous. Today, one-third of all retail stores—95 out of a total of 272—are Chinese-owned and run. These range from mom and pop stores and take-away food shops and auto repair shops to much larger establishment such as grocery stores, medium-sized hotels, taxi companies, and hardware stores. In 2006, Chinese migrants had a 45 per cent share of the total import business licences issued so far that year, or 30 out of 67.

In the late 1990s, Vanuatu also entered the passport business. A Chinese national, Chen Jianpeng, was appointed "honorary consul" to the then still Portuguese enclave of Macau, and Albert Kao, a Taiwan-born Hong Kong resident, was given the same role in the then British colony. Larry

Yu, the director of a Hong Kong-based company called NCI International, which specialised in "investment and immigration services," was appointed Vanuatu's official representative in Cambodia. Yu, who was born in mainland China, carried a passport from the Marshall Islands, and maintained his Cambodia "consulate" in Hong Kong. When asked by Vanuatu's energetic ombudsman, Marie-Noelle Ferrieux Patterson, why he was there instead of in Phnom Penh, Yu replied that it was for "security reasons," as the Cambodian capital was so violent.

In April-May 1997, a four-man delegation from the Vanuatu government, including then foreign minister Willy Jimmy, travelled to Hong Kong and Macau, where their new "diplomatic representatives" presented them with lavish gifts and promises of investment in Vanuatu. More precisely, plans were made to sell passports to Chinese nationals. Cambodia had by then already become an important transit point for illegal migration to the West, a holding centre while fake passports and other documents were being printed in Thailand. A Vanuatu passport could also come in handy somewhere on the way to the final destination, wherever that may be.

A report by ombudsman Patterson put an end to that racket. But in 2000 and 2001, Vanuatu appointed two new "honorary consuls." One of them, a Hong Konger called Chen Hung Kee or Peter Chen, was named Vanuatu's envoy to Britain. He was not unknown to the police. On May 9, 1982, he had organised an armed robbery against a jewellery store in Hong Kong's Wanchai district and escaped with gold and diamonds worth 84,000 US dollars. He was later captured, and in June the following year a court in Hong Kong sentenced him to 15 years in jail. His wife, Lim Suk-wah, received five years. When his criminal record was disclosed, Chen "resigned" as Vanuatu's Hong Kong-based "honorary consul" to Britain.

The other, an Indian living in Thailand called Amarendra Nath Ghosh, was appointed "honorary consul" to Thailand, Laos and Cambodia. His Centurion Bank was registered in Vanuatu, and he was also associated with another offshore bank in the Pacific island republic named GST Bank, which was suspected of having defrauded Banco Ambrosiana

Veneto, an Italian bank, of around 50 million US dollars. Using his newly issued diplomatic passport from Vanuatu, Ghosh applied for a temporary business visa at the Australian Embassy in Bangkok, but was advised to reapply using his Indian passport. However, Ghosh and Vanuatu's then prime minister, Barak Sope, did pay a highly publicised visit to Laos in February 2001. They were received by the Lao prime minister, Sisavath Keobounphanh, and the Vanuatu delegation pledged to invest in "satellite and hydroelectric power" schemes in Laos as well as "telecommunications and eucalyptus planting."

Vanuatu does not have the necessary skills, nor the money, to fulfill those obligations, but exactly what the Vanuatu delegation was up to was not clear. Ghosh was, however, eventually arrested in Germany for having defrauded a number of Indian banks. He tried to swallow a ten-centimetre knife to prevent his extradition to India, but, in August 2007, he was bundled onto a special Indian Air Force plane in Munich and flown back to India after the German authorities had cleared necessary formalities.

Its is not only the necessity to make money in any way they can which makes the Pacific island states prone to exploitation by fraudsters and international tricksters—and far from all of them are of Asian origin. For decades, Australians, British and American tricksters have defrauded the islands through pyramid schemes, promises of international aid that was never delivered, and outright robbery of state assets—and Jesse Bogdanoff, the court jester of Vanuatu, was not the only one. During my first visit to Vanuatu in 1997, I ran into Peter Swanson, a smooth-talking Australian who had persuaded the government to issue ten letters of guarantee, each worth 10 million US dollars, or a total of 100 million US dollars. The letters were deposited in a bank in London, and, if Swanson had managed to use them, the scheme would have bankrupted the entire nation of Vanuatu. Swanson was later deported from Vanuatu. Roddam Twiss, a British confidence trickster, used to run a company called SNIPS, short for "Sovereign Nation Infrastructure Private Sector," which tried to sell "development schemes" to small Pacific nations. But, on order to get what they wanted from international credit institutions, the countries first had to pay vast sums of money into Twiss' own bank accounts. Twiss disappeared without a trace after failing to convince the government of Fiji to "invest" in his "company."

The gullibility of the leaders of the Pacific nations is also astounding, and the combination of these two traits makes the Pacific a perfect playground for Asian and other organised crime. And for illegal migration. An Australian foreign ministry document, which accidentally became public in September 1997, described the leaders of the Pacific island states as "incompetent, drunken, vain and corrupt," and said that their economies "teeter on the verge of bankruptcy." The leakage of the document left embarrassed Australian officials to explain its contents to their smaller neighbours in the Pacific—but although the assessment was harsh, it was not far off the mark. The Pacific island states remain artificial nations and superficially idyllic basket cases with little or no sense of nationhood even for their native inhabitants. It is hardly their fault, but the legacy of decades of exploitation, underdevelopment and a lack of proper education for their citizens.

In 1997 it was revealed that passports from even the relatively well-governed Samoa were being sold under the counter to Chinese businessmen for 26,000 US dollars per document. The scheme was a private initiative, but, once again, showed to what extent people in these small island countries with no natural resources are willing to go to earn money. Apart from passports schemes, many governments in the Pacific have resorted to selling fishing licences to fleets from Japan, Taiwan, South Korea, the United States and now also China, to bring in funds.

More imaginatively, tiny Tuvalu earned 1.2 million dollars, or 10 per cent of its national revenue in 1996, by selling its telephone country-code—688—to American sex hotlines. After that scheme, Tuvalu rented out its catchy country-level domain name on the internet—.tv—first to a Canadian organisation, but when that firm defaulted on payments, the country found a new partner in Idealab, a Pasadena, California capital group and incubator. In 2000, Idealab-incubated DotTV agreed to pay Tuvalu up to 50 million US dollars over

12 years, and not less than 1 million US dollars per quarter, for the right to register .tv Internet addresses. That is quite a lot of money for a country with only 11,000 inhabitants.

The poverty and lack of sophistication of the Pacific island nations makes them vulnerable targets not only for private enterprises but also for penetration by bigger powers, which the diplomatic battles between China and Taiwan clearly show. They are also much more vulnerable when it comes to preserving their national identity than bigger countries such as the United States, Canada, Australia and New Zealand, which receive many more Asian migrants than the Pacific island states. The Asian influence in cities like Sydney and, especially, Auckland is striking.

When I first visited New Zealand, in 1975, there were very few Chinese and those who were there were mostly green-grocers, and most green-grocers seemed to be Chinese. The only fast food available was greasy fish and chips wrapped up in a newspaper. Today, there seems to be nearly as many Asians in the streets of central Auckland as people of European descent—and Asian food courts with cheap but excellent Chinese, Thai, Korean and Indian food abound. According to official statistics, there were 346,000 Asians living in New Zealand in 2003, and that figure is expected to rise to 604,000 or 13 per cent of the population by 2021. There is some resentment among white New Zealanders to this development, but their country can absorb immigrants in a way the smaller island nations cannot. A Chinese living in Australia or New Zealand will became a Chinese-Australian or a Chinese-New Zealander.

Ethnic Chinese have been mayors of Dunedin and Gisborne in New Zealand. In Australia, descendants of Chinese immigrants have been appointed Lord Mayor of Melbourne and Adelaide, and deputy Lord Mayor of Sydney, three of the country's main cities and state capitals. In Canada, people of Chinese origin now make up nearly 10 per cent of the population of British Columbia and 17 per cent in Vancouver city, the province's main population centre. In the 1980s and 1990s, most newly arrived Chinese came from Hong Kong, but in recent years the majority has moved there from the mainland. Chinese is now the third most spoken language in Canada after English and French. An ethnic Chinese former journalist and novelist, Adrienne Clarkson, served as governor-general—or representative of the British Queen—from 1999 to 2005.

But it is not likely that migrants to the Marshall Islands, Tonga or Papua New Guinea will, to the same extent as those in Australia, New Zealand, Canada or the United States, identify themselves with their new host countries, where not even the native population have a clear sense of nationhood. The loyalties and national identification of the migrants will remain with China. Therefore, there is little concern among "migrant businessmen" from China about the destruction of the rain forests of the Solomon Islands and Papua New Guinea, local sensitivities in Tonga, or the need to preserve the marine environment in the Marshall Islands. Politically, it also means that they are likely to put China's strategic interests before those of the smaller nations of the South Pacific, which may want to remain neutral. The United States, France and other Western colonial powers are, of course, no different—but the advent of a new, increasingly powerful China in the region is bound to lead to conflicts of interests, where the Pacific nations will be caught in the middle of a power play over which they have no control or even noteworthy influence.

At the same time, it is important not to resort to racism when discussing the increased Chinese influence in the Pacific. Michael Powles, a former New Zealand ambassador to the Pacific who later headed the New Zealand embassy in Beijing, told the magazine *Island Business* that he had heard one Pacific academic say that "while the Pacific has got used to Western crooks and swindlers over the years, the difference with the Chinese is that they didn't even subscribe to a moral order such as the West's Judeo-Christian inheritance. Had he never heard of Confucius?" Powles argued that everyone has to accept and adapt to the Chinese involvement in the region: "If the region is prepared to take notice of what's happening and take a few sensible measures (like ensuring Pacific countries adopt sensible policies on the issue of visas and passports, and the enforcement of law in respect to itinerant Chinese businesspeople) and look for opportunities which the trend can provide, then there would be as much cause for satisfaction."

Nevertheless, China's influence is increasing at the expense of that of the West's—and it is not only a question of trade, commerce and immigration. Australian academics John Henderson and Benjamin Reilly have stated that, "while the causes of regional instability and conflict in Oceania are mostly internal, it is no accident that China's increased involvement coincides with growing regional instability. The very weakness of Pacific island states makes them vulnerable as a strategic resource for China. Their financial and other problems make the support of Pacific states cheap for Beijing to buy. At the same time, their utility as a source of diplomatic recognition (particularly in the China and Taiwan tussle), voting blocs in international forums, fishing and other maritime resources, and as possible sites for port facilities or even military bases, means that relatively small investments in these countries can have major longer-term payoffs for countries such as China."

US writer Robert Kaplan argued in the June 2005 issue of the *Atlantic Monthly* that the Pacific will become the main arena for a second Cold War between the United States and China that will last for decades. Rather than being "an ocean of peace"—which the Pacific Ocean actually means—it seems destined to be the next arena for super power rivalries, which will inevitably spill over into Australia and mainland Asia. An arms race in the Pacific, for instance, would not leave any major country surrounding the ocean untouched. At the very least, it would be necessary to "choose" which superpower to be the closest too, and that is not a desirable prospect for countries which would prefer to stay neutral.

The third wave of Chinese migration is in full swing, and it is not certain that, in the long run, it will be entirely peaceful and without conflicts in regions such as the Pacific. It is more closely connected to China's strategic interests than previous waves of emigration from relatively isolated areas of Fujian and Guangdong. Strategically, China is making inroads into a region previously dominated by the West, and that is bound to change its entire balance of power. As it may do in the Russian Far East and in certain parts of Southeast Asia.

CHAPTER FIVE
THE GREAT GOLDEN PENINSULA

In the 1990s, Boten, the last town in northwestern Laos before the Chinese frontier, received few outside visitors other than car smugglers. Hondas, built at the Japanese motor giant's plant in the United States, or German luxury sedans bought in Bahrain and other Gulf states, were sent to Bangkok and on through Thailand to the northern town of Chiang Khong on the Thai side of the Mekong river. Then they were ferried across to Ban Huay Xay in Laos and driven in convoys to Luang Nam Tha on the border of China's Yunnan province. There, the traders faced Chinese import duties and other charges that could exceed 200 per cent of the car's value. But less costly arrangements could be negotiated with the border officials. While the smugglers were waiting for the right moment to cross the border, I and a handful of other occasional visitors saw hundreds of cars parked on an open field in the middle of nowhere in the frontier settlement of Boten. Local landowners earned small fortunes renting out parking space to these rather unusual car dealers.

"Exporting" cars to China via Laos in this roundabout way was a booming business, until the late 1990s, when authorities on both sides of the border decided to crack down on the racket. But an alternative source of wealth was soon found for this remote border town in Laos. In October 2002, plans for the Boten Border Trade Area were finalised when the country's then prime minister, Boungnang Vorachit, issued a decree to set up a zone for "the promotion of investment, trade and for creating jobs."

The initial plan was later modified, and a 23 square kilometre zone was created, which was leased to Chinese investors. Local villagers were told to move out, and their wood and bamboo huts were demolished to make way for a three-star, 281-room hotel and casino complex, which opened for business in early 2006. Rates range from 78 US dollars for a standard room to 2,688 US dollars for the hotel's presidential suite. All major credit cards are accepted here—and also in the casino, which has nine gaming rooms with around 50 tables offering baccarat at a minimum of 10,000 Chinese renminbi, or 1,450 US dollars, per hand.

Security guards at the entrance of the casino confiscate cameras and reading material, which are returned when the gamblers leave. A sign behind the front desk prohibits Chinese and Laotian nationals from gambling, although this is clearly not enforced in Boten. Laotians, perhaps, but Chinese can be seen at every gaming table, mixing with Thai gamblers who have arrived by minibus from Chiang Khong and Ban Huay Xay. Prostitutes can also be seen roaming the casino looking for customers, and they are exclusively Chinese; no Lao women are in the trade.

This is where China meets Southeast Asia, and the road from Boten down to Ban Huay Xay and the Mekong river has been upgraded to a highway since the days car smugglers were almost the only ones using it. A bridge is planned on the Mekong, which would provide a direct, unbroken road link between China and Thailand—and on to other destinations in Southeast Asia. The Ban Huay Xay-Boten road, and its extensions in Thailand, are part of a more extensive, Asian highway system that will connect China with its southern neighbours, and establish direct road links between the capitals of Southeast Asia.

Commerce is already thriving, and, in 2008, Chinese investors began to build another, huge casino complex on the Lao side of the Mekong opposite Chiang Saen in Thailand, not far from Chiang Khong and the official river crossing. By 2011, that casino was finished—a massive, gaudy structure overlooking the once placid Mekong river. The Government of Laos gave to a Chinese company called Roman King Group ten hectares of land for 99 years to create this unusual resort in the middle of the wilderness of the Golden Triangle. The days when China supported communist rebel movements in

Southeast Asia are over; now, trade is the main priority. And with trade comes migrants as China expands its southern sphere of economic influence.

Chiang Saen's riparian port has become one of the busiest on the Mekong as a result of a 2000 agreement between China, Laos, Burma and Thailand on commercial navigation along the river. Thailand-based US researcher Matthew Wheeler wrote in the June 2005 issue of *Jane's Intelligence Review*: "Initiated and funded entirely by China at a cost of 5 million US dollars, the project set out to clear obstacles to navigation from the river between Jinghong in Yunnan and Luang Prabang in Laos. Chinese engineers began blasting eleven rapids and shoals in 2002, completing the first of three planned phases of clearance work a year later." That first phase, Wheeler wrote, is "aimed to permit vessels up to 150 dead weight tonnage (DWT) to navigate safely as far as Thailand's Chiang Saen."

However, blasting was halted in June 2002 by the Thai government over concern that the changes in the watercourse might alter the boundary line with Laos. Environmental groups in Thailand also raised the issue of damage to local communities that depended on fishing for their livelihood. But Chiang Saen has become China's gateway to Thailand in the same way as Boten serves as China's main entry into Laos. And it is not only Chinese foodstuff and consumer goods that are coming down the Mekong; in late 2006, China started to use the river as a new oil-shipping route. *Asia Times Online* reported on January 9, 2007: "The maiden journey on December 29 of two Chinese ships carrying oil up the Mekong underscored Beijing's steadfast determination to find alternative routes for transporting oil and gas it imports from the Middle East." The official Chinese news agency *Xinhua* reported on the two vessels carrying a total of 300 tons to Jinghong from Chiang Saen: "Experts say the waterway will serve as an alternative to the Straits of Malacca as a route for oil shipping and help ensure oil supply to Yunnan and southwest China at large."

The ties that bind China with Southeast Asia are becoming stronger by the year and although Thailand, with its strong economy and long history of absorbing outside influences, may be able to handle this, smaller and weaker countries like

Laos, Burma and Cambodia may be in a much more vulnerable position. China's profile and influence in Laos especially have grown steadily over the past few years at the expense of the land- and riparian-locked country's friendship with Vietnam. A similar development has taken place in Cambodia, another close ally of China's longtime rival in the region, Vietnam.

China, referred to by Cambodian Prime Minister Hun Sen in a 1988 essay as "the root of everything that was evil in Cambodia," has emerged as a major donor to the country and, unlike aid from the West, Chinese assistance here as well as in the Pacific comes with no strings attached for promoting democracy and good governance. China is also a major investor in Cambodia, mainly in the garment industry, but also in agriculture, mining, oil refining, metals production, hotels and tourism. Gone are the days when China supported Hun Sen's sworn enemy, the dreaded, Maoist Khmer Rouge. This murderous group was in power from 1975 to 1979, and then, until the mid-1990s, waged a guerrilla war first against the regime that Vietnam had installed when it invaded Cambodia in December 1978 and January 1979, and later against a democratically elected coalition government that came to power following a UN-brokered peace treaty in the early 1990s. China then saw Hun Sen as a puppet of Vietnam, and Hun Sen missed no opportunity to lash out against China.

The situation began to change when Hun Sen ousted his then-coalition partner, royalist leader Prince Norodom Ranariddh, in a June 1997 coup. Cambodia's Western donors were not amused: The US and Germany suspended non-humanitarian aid until a free and fair election was held. Japan, Cambodia's largest donor, said it would halt new projects.

But China came to Hun Sen's rescue. China was the first country to recognise the regime after the coup—and Hun Sen won praise from Beijing for shutting down and expelling Taiwan's liaison office in the capital Phnom Penh. Hun Sen claimed that Taiwan had been covertly supporting Prince Ranariddh's royalist party, Funcinpec. According to longtime Cambodia watcher Julio Jeldres: "Hun Sen's actions opened the door for Chinese influence in Cambodia... In December [1997], China delivered 116 military cargo trucks and 70 jeeps valued at 2.8 million dollars." In February 1999, Hun Sen paid an official visit to China and obtained 200 million US dollars in interest-free loans and 18.3 million US dollars in foreign-assistance guarantees. And then Chinese investors, businessmen and other migrants arrived.

Chinese began to migrate to Cambodia during the days of the ancient Angkor empire. Chou Ta-kuan [Zhou Daquan], Chinese envoy to the court of Cambodia from 1296-97, wrote in his classic *Notes on the Customs of Cambodia*: "Chinese sailors coming to the country note with pleasure that it is not necessary to wear clothes, and, since rice is easily had, women easily persuaded, furniture easy to come by, and trade easily carried on, a great many sailors desert to take up permanent residence." Merchants and carpenters from China also settled in Cambodia, and in 1606 a Portuguese visitor reported 3,000 Chinese living in Phnom Penh, which had become the capital in 1434.

For centuries, Southeast Asia has been known to the Chinese as "the Great Golden Peninsula", a land of milk and honey, beyond the reach of oppressive Emperors in Beijing. Chinese migration to all countries in Southeast Asia escalated with the advent of steamships and upheavals at home in the mid-19th century. But even here they came mainly from the southern provinces of Fujian and Guangdong, with smaller Hakka and Hainanese communities. That has changed, according to Western sinologist William E. Willmott: "The Chinese population in Phnom Penh, now about 200,000, is more heterogeneous than ever before. The five traditional speech groups (Cantonese, Fujianese, Teochew, Hainanese and Hakka) have been joined by recent arrivals from other parts of China, such as dentists and doctors from Shanghai, doctors and architects from Taiwan and businessmen from Hong Kong. Chinese have also come from other parts of Southeast Asia, including doctors from Singapore and local representatives of companies investing in Cambodia. Ninety per cent of foreign investment in Cambodia comes from companies owned by Chinese in Southeast Asia and China."

In 2004, the Cambodian Investment Board approved for the first time more investment from China than any other country. That year Chinese investors accounted for 89 million US dollars of the total 217 million US dollars approved, while

Malaysia—until then the main foreign investor—ran a distant second at 23 million US dollars. In 2005, Chinese companies ploughed more than 450 million US dollars into Cambodia, more than quadrupling the value of total investments over the year before.

Imports of Chinese-made consumer goods have also soared as roads were built linking Cambodia with China through Laos, opening the way for Chinese hawkers and labourers to move south. According to *Asia Times Online* of October 6, 2006, the exact number of recent Chinese migrants to Cambodia is impossible to assess because of the inaccessibility of Cambodia's many remote provincial areas, but "observers estimate the number to be anywhere between 50,000 and 300,000." Newly-built Chinese temples and community halls can be seen in many parts of Phnom Penh and, in 1991, Chinese New Year was celebrated for the first time in almost 20 years. Today, it is a major event in the Cambodian capital.

A major resurgence of Chinese culture has also occurred and Cambodia's largest and most prestigious Chinese school, Duanhua, has more than 10,000 pupils, making it the largest Chinese school in any country where Chinese is not one of the official languages. There is an unmistakable sense of national pride among the new migrants who grew up in a China that is stronger and far more unified than before. But this has also provoked tensions between new-generation migrants and descendants of older settlers, who—as in Fiji and other Pacific islands—also fear that the newcomers' outward display of nationalism could rekindle longstanding suspicions towards ethnic Chinese communities in their adopted countries.

For example, in May 1999, 300 "new" Chinese massed outside the US embassy in Phnom Penh to protest the bombing of the Chinese embassy in Belgrade, as they did in many other countries around the world. A smaller gathering of ethnic Chinese Cambodians, in the country for generations, held a counterdemonstration, heckling the protesters: "You're not our brothers," one yelled, referring to the suffering of Cambodia's Chinese during the Khmer Rouge regime; despite its close links to China, Cambodia's local Chinese were persecuted as "bloodsucking capitalists." The yeller continued: "Your people killed my people during that time."

But such frictions are not likely to upset China's new partnership with Cambodia. As in the Pacific, Chinese aid includes the construction of highly visible symbols of power and, in Cambodia, China has spent millions of US dollars constructing new buildings for the Council of Ministers Building and the National Assembly. That assistance paid off when, in January 2009, the National Assembly approved deals with two Chinese companies—the China Heavy Metal Machinery and the Michelle Corporation—for the construction of four hydro-electric dams in Koh Kong province. The investment is worth more than 1 billion US dollars, China's biggest project so far in the impoverished Southeast Asian nation.

The *Los Angeles Times* summed up China's drive into Cambodia in a September 2006 article: "China's interest in this country—where income per person was 350 US dollars in 2004—is largely driven by the same need that is sending Chinese to remote regions in Africa, Central Asia and South America: to secure natural resources to fuel its expanding economy and enhance its global political muscle."

The same could be said for China's interest in Laos, a country with an even smaller population—6.5 million—and ranked as one of the poorest countries in Asia. And Chinese presence in Laos goes way beyond the casino in Boten. Laos' changing allegiances are reflected in the history of three apartment blocks on the road to the capital Vientiane's Wattay airport. Built in the early 1970s to accommodate operatives of the US Central Intelligence Agency and other American advisers who were there during the Indochina War to support the right-wing, Royal government against communist insurgents and North Vietnamese troops in the country, the buildings were taken over by Soviet technicians when the communist Pathet Lao took over in December 1975. Today, the Mekong Hotel and Apartments cater to a mainly Chinese clientele, with one floor housing the Beijing Restaurant. While Lao national radio and television like to mention the "everlasting friendship" between Laos and Vietnam, China has become the country's main ally.

The number of Chinese working in Laos has increased markedly since the Ban Huay Xay-Boten highway was built. Thousands of Chinese who worked on the road project have remained in Laos and opened shops and restaurants. According to official statistics, about 30,000 Chinese now live in Laos, but the real figure could be ten times greater. At the same time, China has become a major investor in Laos, with 236 projects worth around 876 million US dollars, a considerable increase from 3 million dollars worth of investment in 1996. The total Chinese direct investment approved by Laos' Committee for Planning and Investment up to August 2007 amounts to 1.1 billion US dollars, second only to Thailand's projects worth 1.3 billion US dollars. About a third of the Chinese investment is in hydropower, and the Lao government has granted Chinese companies concessions to mine gold, copper, iron, potassium and bauxite. Vast tracts of land have been farmed out to Chinese interests for rubber plantations.

China's assistance to Laos since the late 1990s has reached nearly 500 million US dollars in grants, interest-free loans and special loans. China has built a huge "Cultural Hall" in Vientiane, ostensibly in traditional Lao style. Some would claim it is a monstrosity and an eyesore in an urban landscape otherwise dominated by French colonial-style villas and modest shop houses. In November 2004, China beautified the park around the Vientiane landmark Patouxay, the capital's Arch of Triumph, and then constructed a stadium for the Southeast Asian games which Laos hosted in 2009.

According to a June 2007 report in the English-language *Vientiane Times*, special loans from China helped establish the Lao Telecom Company and Lao Asia Telecom, and also funded a cement factory, the purchase of two MA 60 aircraft for Lao Airlines, as well as several government internet projects. The Chinese ambassador in Vientiane participates in donors' meetings and plays an active role in the life of Lao-based diplomats. And soon he might be joined by thousands, perhaps tens of thousands, Chinese citizens in a new Chinatown that is being planned for Vientiane. However, for reasons of sensitivity, it is called a "New City Development Project."

If the plan holds, the small and sleepy Lao capital might one day look like Manhattan on the Mekong. An artist's impression in the state-owned media in 2008 shows the shape of a new development that will turn marshland into a modern city—populated by an expected 50,000 migrants from China. According to an April 6, 2008 report by the *Associated Press*, a Chinese company has been granted a renewable, 50-year lease over 4,000 acres for the construction of high-rise buildings and shopping centres. The deal is a spin-off of China's support for the 2009 Southeast Asian games; when the Lao could not afford to built the stadium themselves, they turned to the state-owned China Development Bank for help. The bank offered a Chinese company, Suzhou Industrial Park Overseas Investment Co., a loan to build the stadium in exchange for the lease.

Now, three Chinese companies are reported to be involved in the "New City Development Project"—which, not surprisingly, has become extremely controversial. The *Associated Press* quoted a middle-class Vientiane resident as saying: "The Lao people are not strong so they are afraid the Chinese will come in and expand their numbers and turn our country into China. We will lose our own culture." Unlike Cambodia, which has an outspoken press, the media in Laos in strictly controlled by the government. The middle-class resident also told the Associated Press that, "Lao journalists would like to write about this but they cannot. There is no protest except in coffee shops—in our 'coffee parliaments'." Martin Stuart-Fox, an Australian expert on Laos, added: "The old generation of Lao leaders knew how to balance China's influence and Vietnam's and avoid being crushed between its powerful neighbours. But this generation has passed. It seems to me that the balance is being lost."

Burma, another country squeezed between two powerful neighbours, has also been subjected to China's southward expansion. While Burma's military regime has, until very recent times, been shunned by the West for its abysmal human-rights record and repressive political system, China and India are jockeying for influence in that country. For years, China supported the insurgent Communist Party of Burma, CPB, with weapons, money and even military advisers. But a significant policy shift could be detected as early as on August 6, 1988. On that date, China and Burma signed a border trade agreement—at a time when Burma was in turmoil. Two days later, on the historic day 8.8.88, millions of people in virtually every city, town and village in Burma took to the streets to demand an end to army rule and a restoration of the democracy the country had enjoyed prior to a military takeover in 1962.

The Chinese, renowned for their ability to plan far ahead, had expressed their intentions, almost unnoticed, in an article in the official weekly *Beijing Review* on September 2, 1985. Titled "Opening to the Southwest: An Expert Opinion," the article, which was written by a former vice-minister of communications, Pan Qi, outlined the possibilities of finding an outlet for trade from China's landlocked provinces of Yunnan and Sichuan, through Burma, to the Indian Ocean. It mentioned the railheads of Myitkyina and Lashio in northern Burma, and the Irrawaddy river, as possible conduits for the export of Chinese goods—but it omitted to mention that no relevant border area, at that time, was under Burmese central government control.

The situation changed in 1989, when the hill tribe rank-and-file of the CPB's army rose in mutiny against their ageing, Burman Maoist leaders. The soldiers and their local commanders were mostly Wa tribesmen from the remote and rugged mountains straddling Burma's northeastern border with China. The CPB then controlled a 20,000 square kilometre area along the Chinese frontier, which it seized control of during the late 1960s and early 1970s, when it was China's policy to support communist insurrections in Southeast Asia and elsewhere.

The CPB's leadership and their families, approximately 300 people, fled across the border into China, where they were retired and told to settle in Kunming, Yunnan's provincial capital, and in small border towns such as Ruili, Tengchong and Jinghong. The CPB's 20,000-strong rebel force split along ethnic lines into four different regional armies—and all of them entered into ceasefire agreements with Burma's military government. In exchange for not fighting the central government, they were allowed to retain their armies and control of their respective areas—and to engage in any kind of trade to sustain themselves. By 1990, trade between China and Burma was flourishing, and ties between the two countries— directly and through the so-called "ceasefire armies"— gradually gained strength. Within a few years, Burma became China's principal political and military ally in Southeast Asia.

Chinese arms began to pour into Burma to help the survival of its extremely unpopular military regime, recipient of worldwide condemnation when it brutally crushed the August-September 1988 pro-democracy uprising. Thousands of people were mowed down when the army fired into crowds of unarmed demonstrators. Many more ended up in prisons and labour camps. In view of the Burmese massacre of 1988—and the Tiananmen Square one in Beijing the following year—it was perhaps not surprising that the two then isolated, internationally condemned neighbours would feel a great empathetic bond. On September 30, 1989, Burma's intelligence chief, Lt.-Gen. Khin Nyunt, said in an address to a group of Chinese engineers working on a project in the then capital Rangoon: "We sympathise with the People's Republic of China as disturbances similar to those in Burma last year broke out in the People's Republic of China [in May-June 1989]."

But Burma was strategically important to China as well, as Pan Qi had pointed out in his 1985 article. By late 1991, Chinese engineers and technicians were assisting Burma in a series of infrastructure projects to spruce up the country's poorly maintained roads and railways. Chinese military advisers arrived in the same year, the first foreign military personnel to be stationed in Burma since the Australians had a contingent there to train the Burmese army in the 1950s. And military hardware from China began to arrive. During the first decade after the 1988 uprising, China supplied 80 Type 69II medium battle tanks, more than 100 Type 63 tanks, 250 Type 85 armoured personnel carriers, multiple launch rocket systems, howitzers, anti-aircraft guns, HN-5A surface-to-air missiles, mortars, assault rifles, recoilless guns, rocket-propelled grenade launchers, JLP-50 and JLG-43 air defence radars, heavy trucks, Chengdu F-7M Airguard jet fighters, FT-7 and FT-6 jet trainers, A-5C ground attack aircraft, SACY-

8D transport planes, Hainan-class patrol boats, Houxin-class guided missile fast attack craft, minesweepers and small gunboats. In 2000, China delivered twelve Karakoram-8 trainers-ground attack aircraft, which are produced in a joint venture with Pakistan, another Chinese ally in the region.

The total value of Chinese arms deliveries in Burma in the 1990s is not known, but estimated to be between 1 and 2 billion US dollars. After crushing the 1988 uprising, and to prevent a recurrence of similar popular movements, Burma's military regime has also more than doubled the size of its armed forces. The number of men in the three services increased from 186,000 in 1988 to 450,000 in 2001, and all three branches—the army, the navy and the air force—underwent significant modernisation programmes.

While one of the reasons why China decided to arm Burma may have been to provide a military umbrella to protect new trade routes through potentially volatile territory, the support could also be seen in a more long-term perspective. Access, even indirectly, to the Indian Ocean gives China a strategic advantage. China wants to guard its vital oil supplies from the Middle East through the Strait of Malacca.

Not surprisingly, China's push down to the Indian Ocean has caused considerable concern in its regional rival India, especially the Chinese role in the upgrading of Burma's naval facilities—including at least four electronic listening posts along the Bay of Bengal and the Andaman Sea: Man-Aung on an island off the coast of the western Burmese state of Arakan; Hainggyi Island in the Irrawaddy delta; Zadetkyi, or St. Matthew, Island just north of the entrance to the Malacca Strait; and the strategically important Coco Island just north of India's Andaman Islands. Chinese technicians were also seen at the Burmese naval bases at Monkey Point near Rangoon, and the Kyaikkami facility south of the port city of Moulmein.

Contrary to some alarmist reports in the Indian media about "Chinese bases in Burma," those have remained Burmese bases. But the fact that they were upgraded with Chinese assistance, and that the new radar equipment is Chinese-made—and most likely in the beginning operated at least in part by Chinese technicians—has enabled Beijing's intelligence agencies to monitor this sensitive maritime region.

China and Burma have signed several agreements under which they have pledged to share intelligence that could be of use to both countries. In 2001, a Chinese submarine was spotted visiting the port city of Sittwe in Arakan ahead of a visit by a high-powered Chinese military delegation, adding an important strategic element to Beijing's arms sales to Burma. Those were clearly not just commercial deals.

In June 1998, India's then defence minister, George Fernandes, caused an uproar when he accused China of helping Burma install surveillance and communications equipment on islands in the Bay of Bengal that could be used to spy on Indian naval installations in the region. Burma denied the accusations, while China's foreign ministry expressed "utmost grief and resentment" over the minister's comments. New Delhi, however, had good reason to be concerned. In August 1994, the Indian coast guard caught three boats "fishing" close to the site of an Indian naval base in the Andamans. The trawlers were flying the Burmese flag—but the crew of 55 was Chinese. There was no fishing equipment on board—only radio communication and depth-sounding devices. The crew was released at the intervention of the Chinese embassy in New Delhi. The incident was discreetly buried in the defence ministry files in New Delhi. But when China's designs became more obvious, the government in New Delhi began to pay greater attention to developments in Burma.

In March 1997, China's official *Xinhua* news agency reported that a Sino-Burmese expert group had "conducted a study on the possibility of land and water transport, via Yunnan and into the Irrawaddy valley in Burma." On May 5 that same year, *Xinhua* went on to report that China and Burma had reached an agreement on developing this route, which would be 5,800 kilometres shorter than the older routes of access, which linked Kunming and the nearest, main port on China's east coast, Shanghai. Burmese markets were also flooded with cheap Chinese consumer goods, and China began to import vast quantities of timber from Burma. Large tracts of northern Burma have become almost denuded, and China is now exploring for oil, gas and minerals in Burma as well.

Long before the 1997 agreement was reached, however, China had begun constructing a railway from Kunming to Xiaguan, on its side of the border with Burma. The old Burma Road—built during World War Two by Western Allied powers to supply Nationalist Chinese forces resisting the Japanese— from Kunming to the border town of Ruili was also upgraded, and Chinese engineers extended that road across the frontier to Bhamo on the Irrawaddy River in Burma's Kachin State. Bhamo is the northernmost port on the Irrawaddy that is accessible by boat from the south. The plan is to use a fleet of barges to transport goods from there to Minhla, some 100 kilometres downriver and 280 kilometres north of Rangoon. From Minhla, a road will be built across the Arakan Yoma mountain range, down to Kyaukpyu on the coast. Kyaukpyu was chosen as the site for a new deep-water port rather than the silted mouth of the Rangoon River. On March 27, 2009, Burma and China signed an agreement for the construction of a pipeline that will transport Middle East and African oil from the Arakan coast through Burma to China, short-circuiting the long sea voyage through the Strait of Malacca and via Singapore. A parallel pipeline will tap into Burma's gas reserves in the Andaman Sea. When completed in 2013, the 2.5 billion US dollar project will become a more important conduit for such energy supplies than the ships now plying the Mekong river from Chiang Saen to Jinghong.

In late 2010, the Burmese media reported on Chinese plans to build a railway to connect Kunming with Kyaukpyu— where an industrial zone will also be established. According to the *Eleven News* magazine of October 16, 2010, the railway is expected to be finished in 2015. Another rail route will connect the 1,920 kilometres between Kunming and Burma's former capital and major port Rangoon. According to *Asia Times Online* of Jan 8, 2011, "this route would also link with a railway connecting a new port project in Dawei (Tavoy) on the country's southern coast. A component of the port project... is the construction of a new rail line between Dawei and Bangkok." Thus, an entirely new network of railways, roads and waterways will tie the entire region to Yunnan, and serve Chinese exports as well as imports and other commercial activities. In March 2010, China's official *People's Daily Online* reported that bilateral trade between Burma and China hit US$ 2.9 billion in 2009, an increase of 10 per cent over the previous year and up from virtually zero in the late 1980s. The trade balance weighed heavily in China's favor: in 2009, Chinese exports amounted to US$2.3 billion, while its imports from Myanmar totaled a mere U$646 million. More current trade figures are not publicly available, but are believed to be even higher and still weighted in China's favor.

India's security planners are alarmed at these developments. Before the 1962 military takeover in Burma, independent India had maintained cordial relations with Rangoon. Jawaharlal Nehru and U Nu, the first prime ministers of the two countries, shared a common worldview, and India even lent some military assistance to the government in Rangoon in the upheavals and insurrections that followed on the heels of Burma's independence. Even after the coup in 1962, India kept up formal relations with Burma—until the 1988 uprising and the subsequent, bloody crackdown on the pro-democracy movement. India's prime minister at that time, Rajiv Gandhi, came out in open support of the movement for democracy. India even began to supply some of Burma's many ethnic rebel armies with arms and ammunition. Supporting all these forces was India's way of countering China's growing influence in Burma.

However, around 1993 India began to re-evaluate its strategy out of concern that its policies had achieved little except push Burma even closer to Beijing, and so had the sanctions policy of the West. The result was a dramatic policy shift aimed at improving relations with Burma's military government to lessen its heavy dependence on China. In 2000, the then Indian Army chief, Gen. Ved Prakash Malik, paid a two-day visit to Burma, which was followed by visits to India by Burma's army chief, Gen. Maung Aye. The Indo-Burmese border was opened for trade, and soon it came to rival the trade across the Sino-Burmese frontier. India, like China, has also showed interest in buying oil and gas from Burma.

China has not let go of its upper hand in Burma. Its strategic location and abundance of natural resources—gas, timber and minerals—are too important for China's long-term interests in the region. And even Burma has seen a large influx of immigrant workers, black market traders and gamblers from China. According to the London-based environmental advocacy group Global Witness, 30 to 40 per cent of the population of the northern city of Mandalay is now Chinese. This has caused considerable concern, but in military-ruled Burma any sign of civil unrest in urban areas is quickly suppressed. But ethnic Chinese are known to have been attacked by Kachin tribesmen near Kutkai in the country's northeast. This is especially sensitive as the capital Rangoon was rocked by anti-Chinese riots in 1967. Mobs went on a rampage through the then capital Rangoon's Chinatown, burnt shops and attacked family homes. Those riots were instigated by the government, which at the time was facing anger from the population at large for rising food prices. The Chinese, many of whom where merchants, became convenient scapegoats.

Government-instigated riots against Burma's Chinese now are unlikely, given the regime's dependence on China. But if the economic conditions in Burma continues to deteriorate, spontaneous attacks on Chinese businesses could well occur even in urban areas, where ethnic Chinese now dominate trade and commerce, often in joint ventures with military outfits. The suspension of the Chinese mega-dam in the north of the country in September 2011 may have changed the situation somewhat and the future of Sino-Burmese relations could take a different course. Burma's growing economic and financial dependence on China has caused considerable consternation within its military leadership. Aung Lynn Htut, a former intelligence officer who sought political asylum in the US in 2005, wrote in a September 30, 2011 commentary for exile-run *The Irrawaddy* that the country's military leaders have not forgotten that they once fought against the China-backed CPB and that many of their comrades were killed by Chinese arms.

And, as is the case in Fiji, recent Chinese migration into Burma has also upset local Chinese communities, which fear that they might be targeted as well if there were violent outburst of anti-Chinese sentiments. Most "old" Chinese arrived in Burma during the British colonial era, and nearly all of them settled in urban areas. Many of them were Cantonese, who had come from Calcutta—which until recently had a sizeable Chinese community—or Fujianese, who had migrated from Singapore and what now is Malaysia. The Cantonese were carpenters, shoemakers and skilled artisans, while the Fujianese ran shops and small businesses. But, in the past, the Chinese were never as numerous as the Indians brought in by the British to work as coolies, stevedores, rickshaw pullers and watchmen—and to run the civil service, post offices and the railways. Before World War Two, 45 per cent of Rangoon's population was of South Asian origin—Hindu, Muslim and Sikh.

The Indians came to be deeply resented by the Burmese, as they were the "buffer" between the indigenous population and the colonial power. Anti-Indian riots broke out in Rangoon in the mid-1930s, and, after independence from Britain in 1948, many left for India. Even more Indians returned home when the military seized power in 1962 and nationalised all private businesses. Many Chinese left, too, while significant numbers remained, mostly running the black market that emerged because of the military's mismanagement of the economy.

After the 1988 uprising, Burma's rulers decided to allow free trade and private businesses, and "old" as well as "new" Chinese began to prosper. Burma is also actually unique in Southeast Asia in having not just immigrant Chinese but its own indigenous Chinese minority. These are Chinese who have ended up on the Burmese side of the border with China, in an area known as Kokang, by an accident of history. A mountainous region in Burma's northeastern Shan State, Kokang has always been a buffer zone—or link—between Yunnan and Burma. Although it remained part of China for centuries, its location in a remote corner of Yunnan made it next to impossible for the central government to exercise control over the area. Kokang was left alone, and, over generations, grew a strong sense of independence.

As trade between Yunnan and British Burma began to flourish in the mid-19th century, some of the local chieftains in Kokang prospered. This border buffer was home to both valuable opium and reputedly the best tea in the region. For economic and strategic reasons, the British became increasingly interested in Kokang, and the area was formally ceded to British Burma by the Anglo-Chinese Treaty of February 4, 1897, although its inhabitants were almost exclusively of Yunnanese stock.

After Mao Zedong's victory in the Chinese civil war, thousands of defeated, Nationalist Chinese Kuomintang forces retreated into northeastern Burma. With the help of Taiwan and the United States, they regrouped and were rearmed, and this "secret army" of thousands of soldiers tried on several occasions to re-infiltrate China with the aim of staging an uprising against its new communist government. That did not succeed, and the Burmese army launched several offensives against the unwelcome intruders. In 1961, the Burmese government also turned a blind eye to a massive Chinese military operation. Three divisions of regulars from the People's Liberation Army crossed the border between Sipsongpanna in southern Yunnan and the Kengtung area in easternmost Shan State. The campaign, code-named the "Mekong River Operation," broke the back of the Kuomintang in northeastern Burma, and many of the defeated soldiers retreated down to Thailand.

But some Kuomintang remained in northern areas, where they collected intelligence for Taiwan and the United States. That was one of the main reasons why China in 1968 decided to lend all-out support to the CPB. Burma's communist forces were used to drive out the Kuomintang from Kokang and other areas, which then were taken over by the CPB. Following the 1989 ceasefires, the Kokang Chinese became Burmese citizens after decades of living outside any governmental control. Many Yunnanese from the other side of the border also registered as natives of Kokang, which became a convenient link for migration to Burma. Once across the border and issued with Burmese identification documents, they moved on to Mandalay, Rangoon and other cities to join other Chinese migrants, who had entered the country in other ways, for instance by simply buying ID cards.

An article in the French newspaper *Le Monde Diplomatique* in November 2006 was headlined "Burma: a 24th province for China." That may be an exaggeration, but Burma has, in effect, become a Chinese client state. Ironically, what the old

CPB had failed to achieve for the Chinese on the battlefield has been accomplished by shrewd diplomacy, trade and migration.

Thailand has also received a large influx of new Chinese migrants, and that, too, has partly occurred via remote border settlements. When most of the Kuomintang forces were driven out of Burma in the early 1960s, they settled in the mountains of northern Thailand. The most prosperous of these "Kuomintang" settlements is Mae Salong in Chiang Rai province. Tolerated by the Thai authorities because they were useful as a border security force against Burma, the Chinese in Mae Salong for years maintained their own army. When the Thais in the late 1970s and early 1980s needed battle-hardened troops to fight their insurgents, the Communist Party of Thailand, Kuomintang soldiers from Mae Salong and similar settlements in the north were deployed on battlefields in northern and northeastern Thailand. As a reward for their efforts, many of them were granted Thai citizenship.

But they also planted cherry trees, tea and other crops. Hand-painted Chinese character scrolls around doorways and Chinese-style houses gives Mae Salong a very distinct Chinese character, very different from hill-tribe and Thai villages in the same area. The Chinese schools in Mae Salong and elsewhere in the northern mountains were supported by the Taiwan-based "Free China Relief Service." School textbooks and even teachers were supplied by Taiwan. But those Chinese did not come from Taiwan. They and their ancestors were born in Yunnan or Sichuan; Taiwan was their spiritual and political homeland.

When the Democratic Progressive Party, DPP, won the elections in Taiwan in 2000 and Chen Shui-bian became the president of "the Republic of China," the loyalties of the Chinese in Thailand's northern mountains changed. The DPP was not interested in representing China as a whole, but advocated independence for the island under the name "Taiwan." Thailand's Kuomintang Chinese then realised that they had more in common with the government in Beijing. Communism was in effect dead as an ideology in China; the new, capitalist China had more in common with the freewheeling, capitalist regime of pre-revolutionary days.

Senior Kuomintang commanders began visiting China, and were given red-carpet treatment in Kunming as "war heroes" returning to the "motherland."

And it became easy for migrants from Yunnan to settle in the old Kuomintang villages in northern Thailand, where they could be included in someone's family, and, for a fee, given some kind of Thai identification papers. After a year or so in places such as Mae Salong, they have learnt Thai as well, and can move on to other places in the country. The northern town of Chiang Mai probably has as many recent Chinese arrivals as Mandalay, but, in Thailand, they blend in more easily. And the Chinese in general in Thailand are much more assimilated than elsewhere in Southeast Asia. Thailand's relative prosperity is based on a marriage of convenience between the Sino-Thai plutocracy and the country's military and civil bureaucracy. But the Sino-Thais, who have been in the country for more than a century, had to adapt to Thai ways, take Thai names and send their children to Thai schools.

Today, is it almost impossible to determine how many people of Chinese descent there are in Thailand as intermarriages also have been common. But the old equilibrium can be upset by the flood of new migrants. It is a creeping invasion that a growing number of local Thais are watching with unease. "As a Thai, I feel overwhelmed," a Bangkok-born woman who now lives in Chiang Mai told me. "Of course, Chinese have been moving south for centuries. But we have never seen as many new businessmen, and settlers, as now."

Trade between Thailand and China is also booming, and so are cultural and political exchanges. All this may not affect Thailand in the same way as Laos, Cambodia and Burma— but Thailand no longer can be seen as the same Western ally as it was during the Cold War and the armed conflicts in Indochina in the 1960s, 1970s—and the 1980s, when it was a frontline state against communist-ruled and Vietnamese-backed Cambodia.

And, despite the different degree of Chinese influence in the Southeast Asian countries, they form, in Chinese strategic thinking, one entity. Burma, because of its isolation and being shunned by "human-rights conscious" Western nations may have been the easiest country in the region to penetrate—but Burma is also now showing signs of reasserting its independence and traditionally neutralist foreign policy. But China will always be there, and Burma is unlikely to shake off its dependence on its powerful northern neighbour.

The economic weakness of Laos, and Cambodia's need to rid itself of commercial and political influence from its more powerful neighbours, Thailand and Vietnam, have also worked to China's advantage. Thailand may be more independent, but is also leaning increasingly towards China, which is hardly surprising given the large and economically powerful Sino-Thai business community. China's star is rising in Southeast Asia, and Beijing is rapidly replacing the United States as the region's main superpower. And the highway from Boten to Thailand and beyond has firmly connected China with the Great Golden Peninsula.

CHAPTER SIX
HEAVEN AND EARTH

"You have to understand," the old man said. "We're like the Mafia, but not that bad." I had managed to arrange a meeting in a Southeast Asian capital with a leading member of the Hong Men secret society. He was keen to emphasise that they were not gangsters *per se*, but also philanthropists. They build temples and supported Chinese-language schools. They look after their communities. And, like the people smugglers of Fujian, they are seen by many ordinary citizens as "good people" providing useful services.

If Chinese restaurants are one feature of the world's Chinatowns, Chinese secret societies are another, wrote Shanghai-born author Lynn Pan in her excellent study of the Chinese diaspora, *Sons of the Yellow Emperor*. Secret societies, sometimes referred to as "Triads," have always been endemic to Chinese overseas communities, where they have survived on "protection" rackets. Many would maintain that they thrive on fear and corruption and prosper through their involvement in a wide range of legal and illegal businesses.

For many years, Hong Kong was seen as the "capital" of this worldwide Chinese criminal fraternity and, in the 1980s, many outside observers and analysts thought the gangs based in the then British colony would leave for Canada, Australia and the United States once it reverted to Chinese rule in 1997. The Australian authorities, for instance, thought that 90,000 criminals with links to Chinese gangs would leave as soon as the red five-star flag of the People's Republic was hoisted over Hong Kong.

In the end, the reverse turned out to be the case. Not only did the Hong Kong Triads make arrangements with the territory's new overlords, but they also did likewise in Chinatowns all over the world. New business opportunities in China have spurred Chinese "lodges" and "clan associations" everywhere to forge closer links with the mainland. In China itself, where cutthroat capitalism has replaced the old, austere socialist system, new secret societies, both Triad-linked criminal groups and various syncretic sects, are also expanding at a breathtaking pace.

But no one should actually have been surprised at this development. On April 8, 1993, just as the people of Hong Kong were starting to get used to the idea of a return to the "motherland," Tao Siju, chief of China's Public Security Bureau, gave an informal press conference to a group of television reporters from the territory. After making it clear that "counter-revolutionaries" who had demonstrated for democracy in Beijing's Tiananmen Square in 1989 would not have their long prison sentences reduced, he began talking about the Triads: "As for organisations like the Triads in Hong Kong, as long as they are patriotic, as long as they are concerned with Hong Kong's prosperity and stability, we should unite with them." Tao also invited them to come to China to set up businesses there.

The statement sent shockwaves through Hong Kong's police force and there was an uproar in the media. Since 1845, triad membership had been a crime in the territory, and the rule of law was considered one of the pillars that made it an international city. But it was not a new policy direction taken by the Chinese authorities. Deng Xiaoping, the father of China's economic reforms, had over the years hinted at the existence of connections between China's security services and some Triads in Hong Kong. In a speech in the Great Hall of the People in October 1984, Deng pointed out that not all Triads were bad. Some of them were "good" and "patriotic." The old man I met in the Southeast Asian capital even went as far as claiming that Deng was a sympathiser of the Hong Men society.

While Deng was making those cryptic remarks in Beijing, secret meetings were held between certain Triad leaders and Wong Man-fong, the deputy director of *Xinhua*, the New China News Agency, China's unofficial "embassy" in Hong Kong before the handover. Wong told them that the Chinese authorities "did not regard them the same as the Hong Kong police did." He urged them not to "destabilise Hong Kong" and to refrain from robbing China-owned enterprises. But they could continue their money-making activities.

In the years leading up to the 1997 handover—and especially when the British on Hong Kong's behalf argued for more democratic rights to be included in the territory's proposed mini-constitution, or when the Hong Kong people themselves demonstrated their support for the pro-democracy movement in China—certain "patriotic" Triads were there as Beijing's eyes and ears. They infiltrated trade unions and even the media. Hong Kong—and even China proper—experienced a throwback to Shanghai of the 1930s, when the former rulers of the country, the Kuomintang, had enlisted mobsters to control political movements and run rackets to enrich themselves and government officials alike.

A few days before security chief Tao made his stunning public statement to the reporters in Hong Kong, a new glitzy nightclub called Top Ten had opened in Beijing. One of the co-owners was Charles Heung of the Sun Yee On, one of Hong Kong's most notorious Triad societies—and another was Tao himself.

In the light of such reports, some foreign observers have been quick to jump to the conclusion that "organised crime" and colourful "secret societies" are about to take over China. But Chinese organised crime is not, as many people surmise, a cross between the Free Masons and IBM, well-organised corporate structures shrouded in Masonic ritual. While the criminals may live outside the law, they have never been outside society. In Asia, there has always been a symbiosis between the law and crime—but only with respect to a particular kind of criminal underworld. For instance, organised crime helps the authorities police more unpredictable, disorganised crime to keep the streets safe.

There are also certain things that governments—and big business—just cannot do. A certain company may want to eliminate a competitor, but is unable to do so by normal, legal means. An organised crime gang can then be used to make life difficult for the other party. When in 1984 the Kuomintang security services in Taiwan wanted to get rid of a dissident, troublesome journalist in exile, Henry Liu, they delegated the task to hitmen from the island's most powerful crime syndicate, the United Bamboo gang. The gang was more than willing to carry out the killing, not on account of any concern about Liu, but because in exchange they would get unofficial protection for their own businesses: gambling, prostitution and loan-sharking.

With Taiwan having developed into a democratic—and therefore more transparent—society, the United Bamboo thugs now keeps a much lower profile. But as chaos prevailed in Cambodia in the aftermath of a UN intervention in the early 1990s to restore peace in the war-torn country, the Taiwanese mobsters found a new haven for their activities. Chen Chi-li, nicknamed "Dry Duck" because of his inability to swim as a child, arrived in Phnom Penh in 1996 and whenever new investors from Taiwan came to Cambodia to set up a business, a visit to his luxury villa in the capital was obligatory. Chen's main claim to fame was that it was he who had murdered Henry Liu. After severe pressure from the United States, he was arrested on his return to Taiwan. He received a jail sentence, but was released in 1991.

On July 9, 2000, Chen was arrested in Phnom Penh and charged with possessing firearms, including hand-guns, assault rifles, M-79 grenade launchers and thousands of rounds of ammunition. Many were perplexed, because Chen had managed to be awarded both an honorary royal *Okhna* status—usually acquired through contributions to the state in excess of 100,000 US dollars—as well as an official adviser's position to Cambodian Senate President and security chief Chea Sim.

Not surprisingly, Chen's legal difficulties in his new base turned out to be a minor inconvenience. A year later, Chen was released from custody along with two other suspects. "He used illegal weapons because of fear of his own security," said Cambodian judge Yia Sakom. "The three were not involved with organised crime." Chen's high-level connections were too powerful for anyone in the government, or business, to challenge.

Among other achievements, Chen and his fellow gangsters had turned Cambodia into a clearing house for Chinese migrants who wanted to settle there, or get false documents for their journey to other parts of the world. He continued to live in Phnom Penh until in August 2007 he was hospitalised in Hong Kong, suffering from pancreatic cancer. He died there in October that year, and his body was flown back to Taiwan for burial. Fellow Liu killer Wu Tun, with whom Chen had remained friends, helped to organise his funeral—and over three thousand people came to pay their respects to the gang boss. Among the mourners were politicians, a popular singer, other celebrities—and black-clad teenagers, his storm-troopers who do the dirty work for the gang.

Other gang leaders are closer to mainland China. In late October 2000, Guo Dongpo, director of Beijing's Office of Overseas Chinese Affairs, went to Phnom Penh to see Teng Bunma, a local Sino-Khmer tycoon. Guo wanted his help to control the unruly gangs in the Cambodian capital, who were harassing investors and other businessmen from China. Teng was then not only the honorary president of both the Chinese Association of Cambodia and the Phnom Penh Chamber of Commerce—he was also on Washington's blacklist of suspected drug traffickers, and had been denied entry to the United States.

There are many different, rival Triad societies, and the very first in Chinese history may have been the White Lotus Society, which was founded by monks and scholars in the 12th century and played an important role in the struggle against the Mongol occupation of China in the 13th and 14th centuries. However, most "modern" Triads trace their origin to the *Tiandihui*, "the Heaven and Earth Society," which many believe was set up in the 17th century to overthrow the Manchu Qing Dynasty, and to restore the more indigenous Ming ruling family. Dr Sun Yat-sen, the founder of China's republican movement, capitalised on this popular belief when in the early 1900s he began his struggle against the Manchu emperors. Using the name of the *Tiandihui*, Dr Sun managed to solicit support for his cause among overseas Chinese communities in the Asia-Pacific region as well as in the Ming heartland in southern China, where most Chinese migrants came from anyway. They rallied behind him, although he wanted to establish a republic, not restore the Ming Dynasty.

But more recent research, primarily by American professor Dian Murray, show that the *Tiandihui* was actually set up in the late 18th century—more than a hundred years after the fall of the Ming Dynasty—and then not as a political movement but as a mutual aid organisation in Fujian, then a volatile frontier area. People, especially outcasts and vagrants, needed protection against both bandits and the Emperor's Mandarins, and grouped together in secret societies. The name "Triad," which was coined much later, refers to the magic number "three." Three multiplied by three equals nine and any number whose digits add up to nine is divisible evenly by nine. In Chinese numerology, three was also the mystical number denoting the balance between Heaven, Earth and Man.

Originally, the secret rituals which aspiring members had to go through in order to be accepted into the gangs were meant to bind these tightly-knit brotherhoods closely together in order to avoid betrayal by fellow members of the group. Each society, or lodge of a larger society, was headed by a *shan zhu*, or "Mountain Master," assisted by a *fu shan zhu*, or "Deputy Mountain Master." These two men were frequently referred to as *da lao* (*tai lo* in Cantonese, the language more commonly spoken by the Triads), "Elder Brother" and *er lao* (*yee lo* in Cantonese), "Second Elder Brother."

After the two elder brothers came two officials of equal standing: the *xiang zhu* (*heung chu* in Cantonese) or "Incense Master," and the *xian feng* (*sin fung*) or "Vanguard." These two controlled the Rites Department and were responsible for its elaborate initiation ceremonies. Every new member of the Triad society had—and to this day still has—to obey a series of 36 oaths. The penalty for breaking any of these has, since the formation of the *Tiandihui*, been the same: death. Oaths were sealed by drinking a mixture of blood and rice wine.

Today, these rituals serve as useful means to discipline young hoodlums. By going through "the Gates of Hong"— which Hong Men means—they have sworn to obey their leaders and it also gives them a sense of self-importance. The rituals have remained more or less the same over the centuries, although fear of catching AIDS has forced new recruits in modern times to slit their own finger tips simultaneously and suck only their own blood rather than following the age-old initiation rite of drinking the mingled blood of the aspirants from a communal tumbler.

In the same way as in Fujian, Chinese labourers in Singapore, Penang, Honolulu, San Francisco, Samoa and Tahiti also needed protection in an often hostile environment, and the secret societies were able to fulfill that role. Much later, the *Tiandihui* claimed patriotic credentials and it is also clear that Dr Sun and other Chinese nationalists played up that aspect of the Triads in order to make use of their muscle to further their political goals.

As a result, after the overthrow of the Qing Dynasty of the Manchus in the 1911 revolution, ties between the Triads and the new Kuomintang government were also very close. Dr Sun's successor, Chiang Kai-shek used a group called the Green Gang, led by the notorious gangster Du Yuesheng or "Big-Eared Du," to control leftist trade unions and the communists in Shanghai in the 1930s. To express their gratitude, the Kuomintang authorities in Taiwan later erected a statue in honour of "Big-Eared Du" in Xizhi village near Taipei. The four-character inscription on the monument praises the late Du's "loyalty" and "personal integrity."

In the 1940s, new Triads were set up by Kuomintang officers and the nationalist government's secret police to fight the communists more effectively. The best known was the 14K Society, founded in 1947 by a Kuomintang general, Kot Sio-wong. The gang's name came from its first headquarters, which were located at No 14, Po Wah Road in Guangdong's provincial capital, Guangzhou.

When the communists emerged victorious from the civil war against the Kuomintang in 1949, General Kot fled to Hong Kong with hundreds of his followers. Many of them settled in Rennie's Mill, a run-down village on Junk Bay east of the old Kai Tak airport, where flags of the Republic of China flew over the shabby-looking houses until the entire neighbourhood was "sanitised" in time for the 1997 handover. But the 14K remains one of the territory's most important Triads, with offshoots all over the world.

Heung's Sun Yee On, of all the Hong Kong Triads, seems to have established a very special relationship with the new authorities in Beijing. It is also the only Triad that has computerised membership records, and what appears to be a centrally-controlled structure. That cannot be said of the first "mainland" Triad in modern times, the Dai Huen Jai, or the Big Circle Boys, which has got much more attention from the popular media mainly because it was founded in the 1970s by former Maoist Red Guards who had failed to integrate into society once China's tumultuous Cultural Revolution in the 1960s was over. The name "Big Circle Boys" has cropped up in Hong Kong, Macau, Canada and even the United States. But, like the 14K, it is a name used by many different groups of mainland hoodlums with no central leadership. Some members of the Big Circle Boys may have their personal contacts with people within China's security services, but these are not on the same level as the relationship between the Sun Yee On and the Chinese authorities.

Lao Da, the godfather of the Chinese criminal underworld in the Far East, may fall into the same category of new mainland gang leaders as those of the Big Circle Boys—but his gangs are more closely related and coordinate their activities. And Lao Da is definitely well connected in northeastern China as well as in the Russian Far East.

New gangs have also sprouted in the Pacific as more Chinese have settled there. Most migrants are, needless to say, not criminals but simply people looking for business opportunities and a better future for themselves and their families. But they cannot escape the Triads, whose services are needed to get false passports, arrange residence permits—and to transfer money through the underground Chinese banking system. And the arrival of the Triads means that more serious crime has come to the Pacific as well.

The massive seizure of 357 kilogrammes of Southeast Asian heroin in Fiji in November 2000 was not the only drug haul in the Pacific nation. John Murray, an Australian Federal Police officer who has spent a long time in the Pacific, wrote in his 2006 book *The Minnows of Triton: Policing, Politics,*

Crime and Corruption in the South Pacific Islands: "Chinese Triad connections also figured in a similarly successful police operation that put an abrupt halt to the planned manufacture in Fiji of crystal methamphetamine. When police raided a clandestine laboratory at Laucala Beach in June 2004, they located chemicals capable of producing over a tonne of "ice" with the potential street value of 560 million US dollars. Destined for sale to markets in the USA, Europe, Australia and New Zealand, it also resulted in the arrest of six persons each in Fiji and Malaysia and one in Hong Kong."

In April 2005, Yan Xiu Hua, a woman commonly known as "the Mafia Queen," was deported from Fiji. She had been linked to prostitution rackets, loan sharking, immigration scams, drug dealing, money laundering and other serious organised crime. According to Brian Orme, a colourful Irishman living in Kiribati, whom I met in Suva, the Mafia Queen brought in no fewer than 400 Chinese prostitutes to Fiji. At night, they could be seen, scantily clad, strolling up and down the capital's Victoria Parade, looking for customers. Or they worked from karaoke bars, run by the 'Queen' herself or other recently arrived Chinese migrants. It was such activities—and drug smuggling—that caused concern among Fiji's old-time Chinese population.

Yan had arrived from Hong Kong in 1990 and managed to obtain Fijian citizenship. But it was revoked because she failed to mention in her application for citizenship that she had been convicted for forgery in Hong Kong in 1987. At the time Yan was put on a plane back to China. Fiji's Minister for Home Affairs, Josefa Vosanibola, said: "She has consistently demonstrated that she will not hesitate to carry out her business interests outside the law. And her removal acts as a reminder to illegal immigrants in Fiji and those that subscribe to engaging in illegal activities during their stay."

It was a rather strange statement. So illegal immigrants can stay as long as they do not engage in other illegal activities? The inexperience of the tiny police forces in the Pacific is sometimes startling; often they do not have the necessary resources to tackle organised crime of any sort. Long a haunt of buccaneers, beachcombers and missionaries, the South

Pacific in the 1990s became a new kind of paradise—for crooks, smugglers and money launderers.

The best-established South Pacific tax haven is Vanuatu, formerly the Anglo-French condominium of the New Hebrides. When I first visited its one-street capital, Port Vila, in 1997, the place abounded with nearly 80 banks, numerous insurance agents, accountants, lawyers and 2,000 "shell companies"—entities with no proper office, no staff and which do not produce anything but have been set up solely to be conduits for dirty money, using a solicitor's office as their "local" address. Although some of these businesses were legitimate, Australian officials I interviewed believed that millions of dollars worth of dirty money, including drug proceeds, were placed in the banks of Vanuatu and other Pacific tax havens through trusts and shell companies, protected by a web of impenetrable laws.

Vanuatu actually became a tax haven by default. Before independence in 1980, it was administered jointly by Britain and France—which meant that they could not agree on anything, not even on which side of the road cars should be driven. The "condominium" became the "pandemonium" in popular speech and, consequently, there was no taxation law. After independence, the tax haven was promoted to produce an income for yet another country with few natural resources and a small population.

Vanuatu has the advantage of being in the same time zone as East Asia, so most of its clients came from that part of the world. Moreover, Vanuatu had no reciprocal-tax agreement with any other country, and considered breach of confidentiality a criminal act. Further, as Tim Morris from Australia's financial authority, the Australian Transaction Reports and Analysis Centre, or AUSTRAC, and an expert on money laundering, told me in Sydney: "It's not the absence of taxes, or even the ability to walk into a bank with a suitcase full of cash with no questions asked, that makes offshore banking centres attractive. It's the strict bank secrecy, the inability of any government to investigate the source of unusual wealth parked in places like that."

Concerns about Vanuatu's secretive banking laws was highlighted in 1996 by a scandal in Indonesia surrounding

Vanuatu-incorporated Dragon Bank. The bank, whose abandoned "headquarters" in Port Vila I visited a year later, a small downstairs room in a modest office building, had announced plans for a 101-storey skyscraper in Indonesia's capital Jakarta, a 4 billion US dollars telecommunications venture, also in Indonesia, and an 80 million US dollars property project on the Malaysian island of Langkawi. But in June 1996 government officials in Indonesia shut down Dragon Bank for operating in the country without a licence. In January 1997, a few months before I got there, the government in Port Vila also revoked its banking licence in Vanuatu.

Although the vast majority of Vanuatu's banks were owned by ethnic Chinese from Indonesia, Hong Kong, Taiwan and China, dirty money from other parts of the world also ended up there. Alarm bells rang at AUSTRAC's Sydney headquarters in 1996 when it was discovered that seven Russian banks had shown interest in opening representative offices in Vanuatu. Nauru, Samoa, the Cook Islands, Tonga, Niue and the Marshall Islands have also, at various points in time, provided offshore services for foreign companies and banks, including Chinese and Russian.

But most of these services came to an end after the September 11, 2001 attacks in the United States, and an all-out American offensive against tax havens which served as conduits for money for terrorists or organised criminals, or both. When I returned to Vanuatu in 2005, there were only half-a-dozen offshore banks left. Under Western pressure, a new banking law had been introduced in 2002 which had made money laundering much more difficult. Further restrictions on the world's "tax havens," including those in the Pacific, followed in the wake of the worldwide economic meltdown, which began in 2008. In February 2009, the Cook Islands abolished its law permitting offshore banks to operate in the territory, mainly because of the troublesome activities of the grandly-named Wall Street Banking Corporation—which had nothing to do with Wall Street, New York, but was run by foreign exchange dealers in Dubai, the United Arab Emirates.

Before that, on October 25, 2005, the daily *Cook Islands News* had rather enthusiastically but not very realistically reported that the territory's police force was going to crack down on "any slight trace of Chinese organised crime... that is already menacing other small Pacific island states." The newspaper report stated that those states had become "stepping stones" for thousands of Chinese seeking to enter Australia through immigration scams organised by transnational crime syndicates. The Cook Islands were relatively safe, the article stated, but "so far this year" a number of incidents had take place elsewhere in the Pacific: "Papua New Guinea recently conceded that 'Chinese Mafia' had bought bureaucrats 'throughout the system' and tried to kill people who crossed them; three ethnic Chinese businessmen have been killed in Vanuatu." And then there was, the year before, the massive seizure of methamphetamine-producing equipment and chemicals in Fiji.

So even without tax havens, the Pacific islands have had more than their fair share of criminal activities. And passports can still be bought, people smuggled, and companies, individuals and even governments defrauded— as demonstrated by the activities of Jesse Bogdanoff, the Court Jester of Tonga, and Vanuatu's peregrinating "diplomat," Amarendra Nath Ghosh.

However, there is no evidence linking Chinese criminals in the Pacific to the authorities of their home country—which to some extent is the case in Cambodia, and, even more so, in Burma. The 1989 mutiny in the insurgent Communist Party of Burma, CPB, opened the way for an entirely new relationship between Chinese authorities, Chinese companies, and the Golden Triangle's drug lords, both from Kokang and the wild Wa Hills straddling the frontier. While China supplied the Burmese government with vast quantities of military materiel, it has also maintained cordial relations with the former communist forces. This is hardly surprising, given the long-standing relationship China has had with local rebel commanders in the area.

Most of the CPB's former base area along the Chinese frontier is controlled by the United Wa State Army, UWSA, which the US State Department has described as the largest armed drug-trafficking organisation in Asia. And the UWSA's 20,000-strong force is armed with new Chinese weapons, not old guns left over from CPB days. The ceasefire agreements with the central government are still holding, but to prepare for the possibility of renewed hostilities, the UWSA has in recent years taken delivery of newer and heavier weapons from China. *Jane's Intelligence Review* reported in its March 2008 issue: "As the possibility of war with the [Burmese] junta has loomed larger, the UWSA has acquired more sophisticated weapons, including anti-aircraft systems. In or around 2000 the Wa added to their small arsenal of Soviet Strela-2 (SA-7) man-portable air defense systems when they acquired HN-5N systems, an improved Chinese version of the first-generation Soviet system."

In addition, the UWSA have acquired 12.7 and 14.5 mm anti-aircraft guns, 60 mm, 82 mm and 120 mm mortars. In 2007, advisers from the Chinese People's Liberation Army (PLA) provided training in the use of 122 mm and 130 mm artillery in the Lu Fang mountain range west of the UWSA headquarters at Panghsang, across the border from Meng A in Yunnan. The UWSA's artillery regiment has been equipped with 130 mm field guns, 122 mm howitzers and its soldiers have dug a complex of underground command centers near Panghsang, clearly intended for protection against aerial attacks by the Burmese air force.

The possibility of war between the cease-fire groups and the central government moved closer to reality when, in October 2004, Burma's until then powerful intelligence chief, Gen. Khin Nyunt, was purged and subsequently arrested. Khin Nyunt's ouster was not, as some reports in the foreign media at the time suggested, a power struggle between the "pragmatic" intelligence chief and "hardliners" around junta chief Gen. Than Shwe and his deputy, Gen. Maung Aye. According to the press reports, Khin Nyunt favoured a dialogue with the country's pro-democracy movement and held "moderate" political views. Khin Nyunt may have been smoother in his dealings with foreigners, but his dreaded military intelligence service, the Directorate of the Defense Services Intelligence (DDSI), was the junta's primary instrument of repression against the pro-democracy movement. During the August-September 1988 uprising, he had cracked down on the demonstrators, and had student activists imprisoned, tortured and even killed.

A more plausible explanation for the purge was that Khin Nyunt and his DDSI had accumulated significant wealth through involvement in a wide range of commercial enterprises—and with close links to the UWSA and other cease-fire groups. Khin Nyunt and his men were building up a state within a state and not sharing their riches with the rest of the military elite. And Than Shwe did not want to have any potential rivals around him; Khin Nyunt also clearly had political ambitions. He was a man not to be trusted.

Immediately following the ousting of Khin Nyunt, his latest intelligence outfit, the Office of the Chief of Military Intelligence (OCMI), was dissolved and an entirely new organization established: the Office of the Chief of Military Affairs Security (OCMAS), which was placed under more direct military control. Details of the new military intelligence apparatus remain sketchy, but it is not believed to be as efficient as its predecessors. Some observers even argue that the regime's inability to prevent the emergence of a massive anti-regime movement in September 2007, when tens of thousands of Buddhist monks took to the streets in the old capital Rangoon, would not have been possible if Khin Nyunt and his men had remained in charge of security.

It was Khin Nyunt who had, out of necessity, negotiated the ceasefire agreements with the former CPB forces and other rebel groups in 1989. Suddenly, there was no longer any communist insurgency in Burma, only ethnic rebel armies. The break-up of the CPB also came at a time when central Burma was in turmoil. The protests of 1988 had shaken Burma's military establishment, and it responded fiercely. The crushing of the 1988 uprising was more dramatic and much bloodier than the better publicised events in Beijing's Tiananmen Square a year later.

In the wake of the massacres in Rangoon and elsewhere in the country, more than 8,000 pro-democracy activists fled the urban centers for the border areas near Thailand, where a multitude of ethnic insurgencies, not involved in the drug trade, were active. Significantly, the main drug-funded force operating along the border, Khun Sa and his Möng Tai Army (MTA), refused to shelter any dissidents who had fled the urban areas; his main interest was business, not to fight the government.

The Burmese military now feared a renewed, potentially dangerous insurgency along its frontiers: a possible alliance between the ethnic rebels and the pro-democracy activists from Rangoon and other towns and cities. But these Thai border-based groups—Karen, Mon, Karenni, and Pa-O—were unable to provide the urban dissidents with more than a handful of weapons. In 1988 none of the ethnic armies could match the strength of the CPB, with its then still strong army and relatively large base area along the Sino-Burmese border in the northeast. Unlike the ethnic insurgents, the CPB also had vast quantities of arms and ammunition. The communists were not as strong as before, but they had a substantial arsenal, left over from the aid that China had provided in the 1960s and 1970s. It was enough for at least ten years of guerrilla warfare against the central government in Rangoon.

Despite government claims of a "communist conspiracy" behind the 1988 uprising, there was at that time no linkage between the anti-totalitarian, pro-democracy movement in central Burma, and the orthodox, Marxist-Leninist leadership of the CPB. However, given the strong desire for revenge for the bloody events of 1988, it is plausible to assume that the urban dissidents would have accepted arms from any source. Thus, it became imperative for the new junta that had seized power on September 18, 1988—the State Law and Order Restoration Council (SLORC)—to neutralize as many of the border insurgencies as possible, especially the CPB. With the 1989 mutiny, the situation became even more precarious for Burma's military government, as an alliance between the urban dissidents, the "old" ethnic armies—and the "new" ones, which emerged after the collapse of the CPB—could have become reality.

The mutineers were made an offer. In exchange for not fighting the government's forces—and no alliance with other ethnic rebels—the former CPB forces were allowed to engage in any kind of trade. In those remote border mountains, that meant drugs. In the late 1980s, Burma's opium production suddenly more than doubled as a result of the cease-fire agreements with the former CPB forces. According to the

United States government, the 1987 harvest for Burma yielded 836 tons of raw opium; by 1995, production had increased to 2,340 tons. Satellite imagery showed that the area under poppy cultivation increased from 92,300 hectares in 1987 to 142,700 in 1989 and 154,000 in 1995. By the mid 1990s, Burma's opium production reached 2,000 tons, up from 350-600 tons annually before the CPB mutiny. Furthermore, the cease-fire agreements with the government also enabled the former CPB forces to bring in chemicals, mainly acetic anhydrite—which is needed to convert raw opium into heroin—by truck from India. Within a few years of the mutiny, intelligence sources were able to pinpoint at least 17 new heroin refineries in Kokang and adjacent areas, six in the Wa Hills and two in the mountains north of Kengtung, where the town of Möng La, opposite Daluo in Yunnan, developed into one of the most important drug-running centers in the country.

The heroin trade took off with a speed that caught almost every observer of the Southeast Asia drug scene by surprise. It takes 10 kilograms of raw opium to make one kilogram of heroin, and after deducting the amount of opium that is usually smoked locally, Burma's potential heroin output soared from 54 tons in 1987 to 166 tons in 1995, making drugs the impoverished and mismanaged country's only growth industry. In recent years, opium production has come down to pre-1980s levels—but, instead, methamphetamines are now being produced in northern and northeastern Burma.

Within days of the ouster of Khin Nyunt, Burmese military leaders met with the ceasefire groups, assuring them that nothing was going to change. That was not quite the case. In the UWSA's "capital" Panghsang and other strongholds, posters with pictures of Khin Nyunt and UWSA leader Bao Youxiang walking hand in hand were taken down. Drug laboratories on the Thai border were moved to more secure locations near Panghsang. It was clear that relations between the ceasefire groups and the central government were deteriorating. The central government would like to see the ceasefire groups disarm and transformed into political parties and "local police forces"; the Was and other ethnic groups had no intention of giving up what they had gained through decades of fighting, nor the 1989 agreements with the central government.

Thus, China's policy towards the UWSA—and Burma—is by no means clear-cut. On the one hand, it supports the government—now ensconced in the new capital Naypyidaw—and has blocked Western attempts to bring the Burma issue to the attention of the UN's Security Council. But, on the other, Beijing clearly sees a strategic benefit from maintaining a buffer zone between its border and Burma's characteristically erratic ruling generals and it has various strategic and economic interests in maintaining the UWSA's dominance over the area.

Beijing also fears that a weakened UWSA could invite the Burmese army to launch an offensive, which would risk spilling into China's adjacent Yunnan province and potentially create a refugee situation similar to that in Thailand, where more than 100,000 ethnic Karen, Karenni and Mon have sought shelter from Burma's civil war.

It is unclear if the UWSA had to pay in full for its new Chinese weapons, or if they were sold at friendly prices by the People's Liberation Army. But in order to raise more money, for arms purchases and for running its administration, the UWSA has also moved into regional arms trade. Until recently, most of the arms the UWSA sold to other regional insurgent groups were procured through Yunnan's underground markets, where ex-PLA personnel are known to have sold off munitions stockpiles without Beijing's approval. These activities intensified in Yunnan in the wake of Beijing's ambitious modernization campaign for its armed forces, which included strict orders for provincial PLA members to abandon their private business interests, including arms trading.

While various PLA units were reshaped and re-equipped, many others, particularly in far-flung Yunnan, were reluctant to hand in officially retired arms because of their black-market value in conflict-ridden neighbouring Burma. The UWSA has long been involved in the lucrative underground regional arms trade, which according to security analysts has surpassed Cambodia's notorious arms bazaars in trade volume. In recent years, the UWSA is known to have sold assault rifles and explosives to various rebel groups, including the Naga along India's northeastern border with

Burma, as well as possibly also the Maoist rebels, who in 2008 fought their way into government in Nepal. According to one Bangkok-based security analyst monitoring the situation: "The UWSA couldn't care less about the various ideologies of the groups they supply. They will continue to sell (arms) to whoever wants them as long as they don't expect to face off with the buyers in the near future."

In June 2008, *The Sentinel*, a daily published in northeastern India, reported that the UWSA "is playing a major role in the trafficking of Chinese arms to the North-East." The paper quoted an Indian intelligence source as saying that Chinese automatic rifles, which are available in Burma for 500 US dollars each, are sold in northeastern India for 2,500 US dollars a piece. When the United States put pressure on China to halt counterfeiting of DVD movies and music cassettes, the equipment for producing these were moved across the border to the UWSA-controlled area, beyond any official governmental control. Thailand and the rest of Southeast Asia is now being flooded with counterfeited goods originating in the wild and remote mountains of northeastern Burma.

The UWSA's attempts at strengthening its finances by diversifying its commercial activities thus represent a clear threat to regional security—quite apart from the menace caused by the continuing flow of drugs into Burma's neighbouring countries. But so far only the West seems to be interested in the issue. None of Burma's energy-hungry neighbours wants to antagonise the regime in Naypyidaw, which is sitting on a wealth of natural gas. Thailand already is a buyer, and, as we have seen, China has also invested in Burma's energy sector, apart from benefiting from a booming cross-border trade in consumer goods.

It may seem odd that China, which now has a huge and growing drug problem, would ally itself with a drug-running, criminal gang like the UWSA. But that is the case. The UWSA's *de facto* buffer state between China and government-held areas in Burma has created what amounts to an unrecognised criminal republic that both Burma and China conveniently can claim they do not control.

The UWSA is not a Triad, or even a Triad-type organisation; it is a former rebel army that has made peace with its former enemy, the Burmese government, and managed to retain a great deal of autonomy over the area it controls. But the UWSA can do things for the Chinese authorities that the Chinese just cannot do themselves, so the relationship between the Wa leadership and China is of a similar nature. And, like the Secret Societies, the UWSA has also built temples, schools and hospitals. In the eyes of many locals in their base area, the UWSA leaders may be seen as "good people"—and, at least by parts of the Chinese establishment, they are perceived as a useful force for strategic and commercial purposes. The old policy of maintaining a symbiotic relationship between officialdom and certain types of organised criminals is still very much alive.

But it is not only armed groups such as the UWSA in remote corners of Southeast Asia that are a major cause of concern. Chinese gangs with money and influence are active all over Asia and the Pacific, and the new face of Chinese organised crime, which has followed China's economic expansion and migration, is bound to have a profound impact on regional security. Gone are indeed the days of the "Robin Hoods"—the flamboyant gangsters from Hong Kong and Taiwan with their meat cleavers and scarred faces. They live on only in popular culture and movies. An entirely new breed of entrepreneur is emerging on the fringes of China. The business-like and well-connected suit-wearing managers of the Sun Yee On have shown where the future lies. And gangsters such as Lao Da in the Russian Far East are breaking new ground, which could have far-reaching consequences for the stability of the entire region.

CHAPTER SEVEN
THE SPYING GAME

It was Taiwan's biggest coup in the Pacific. On November 7, 2003, the foreign minister in Taipei, Eugene Chien, announced that "the Republic of China and the Republic of Kiribati have established diplomatic relations." Kiribati may consist of little more than a collection of low-lying atolls spread out over a huge area in the South Pacific—but, more importantly, it was also where China had established a satellite tracking station, the only one of its kind outside the mainland. Kiribati, which straddles the Equator, is an ideal place for satellite tracking.

Within days of the announcement, China vacated its embassy in Tarawa, the capital of Kiribati, and began dismantling the tracking station. Diplomats from Taiwan moved into their new embassy building in Bairiki, a narrow sliver of land on the chain of islets that make up Tarawa atoll. It is not a particularly attractive place. The lagoon is full of rubbish and serves as the atoll's latrine. A third of Kiribati's population of about 100,000 people live in shabby-looking, open-sided huts on the crowded, western tip of Tarawa. But it was strategically important to China, which, apart from gaining one more diplomatic ally in the Pacific, was one of the reasons why Taiwan decided to snatch Kiribati from Beijing.

Kiribati, which was formerly known as the Gilbert Islands, became independent from Britain in 1979 and, a year later, established diplomatic relations with China. Relations between the Asian giant and the Lilliputian nation in the Pacific grew gradually closer. An agreement on "economic and technical cooperation" was signed in June 1983, and, from June 27-July 2, 1985, Kiribati's then president, Ieremia Tabai, paid an official visit to China. His host and Chinese counterpart, Li Xiannian, stated during their meeting in Beijing: "China sincerely hopes that peace and stability will prevail in the South Pacific region. Whatever we do is for peace and stability in the region and for continued growth of the mutually beneficial cooperation between China and the countries in the region. We seek nothing but friendship and cooperation. We have no intention to compete in the region with any country."

The satellite station was set up in 1997 and, in October 2003, the facility helped track the first Chinese man in space, the 38-year-old Yang Liwei. It was a triumph for Chinese technological might and could not have been as successful as it was without land support from Tarawa. It was also long suspected that the Tarawa station was used by China to monitor American missile tests at nearby Kwajalein Atoll in the Marshall Islands. Vital for the development of the United States' missile-defence system, Kwajalein has since 1958 been the target site for inter-continental ballistic missiles launched from California. In more recent years, the United States has conducted missile defence tests and space surveillance activities from Kwajalein.

The removal of the Chinese station in Tarawa came four months after a general election, which was won by Anote Tong, the son of a Chinese immigrant who had settled on the islands after World War Two, and a local woman. His election campaign—and also that of the rival party led by his younger brother, Harry Tong—was reported to have been financed by Taiwan. Both the Taiwanese government and Anote Tong denied the accusations, but Harry Tong went public, claiming that he had received 80,000 US dollars in cash from Taiwan for the campaign. The money, he said, had been paid by Taiwan's trade office in Suva, Fiji, and hand-carried back to Kiribati by his campaign manager and political adviser, Brian Orme, an Irishman who had become a naturalised Kiribati citizen.

I met Brian Orme in Suva a couple of years after the controversial election in Kiribati. He took me around the town's bars. Every beefy Fijian bouncer seemed to know him quite well, addressing him by name, "Mister Brian." Wiry, mustachioed and covered in tattoos, he was in his mid-70s but still strong and active despite his obvious fondness for drink.

Orme was also fairly typical of a certain kind of Westerner who has washed up on Pacific shores. He left home in Ireland in his teens and worked as a merchant seaman before serving with the Canadian contingent in the Korean War in the early 1950s. He then became a mercenary in Africa under the notorious "Mad" Mike Hoare, a fellow Irishman whose first action was in Katanga, a province that broke away from the newly independent Congo in 1960. Hoare's nickname "Mad" Mike comes from broadcasts by Communist East German radio during the fighting in the Congo. The East Germans would precede their commentaries with "The mad bloodhound, Mike Hoare." After leaving Hoare's private army of mercenaries, Orme did a stint as a labour recruiter in Hong Kong, and eventually settled in the then Gilbert Islands in the 1960s. Hoare was later, in 1978, involved in an abortive coup attempt in the Seychelles in the Indian Ocean. Some Europeans, it seems, are much more unscrupulous when it comes to interfering in the internal affairs of small island nations.

Orme, a somewhat unlikely adviser to a politician anywhere in the world except in the Pacific, said that he had gone to Fiji several times to see the Taiwanese representative in Suva, who also had sent him faxes with promises of support. It may sound odd, given that it was the elder brother, Anote Tong, who established relations with Taiwan, that it was the losing candidate, the younger Tong, who admitted that he had received money from the Taiwanese before the election. But Orme suspected that Taiwan must have given money to both sides. He did not believe that Kiribati's new government would have recognised Taiwan without a similar, or perhaps even more generous, contribution to the elder Tong's election campaign. "If you want to know who's going to win the next election, ask Taiwan," Orme told me in Suva, and the same quote from him appeared in a May 9, 2006 story in the *Wall Street Journal*. Anote Tong was re-elected in October 2007, for a second term.

While denying that he personally received money from Taiwan, the new Kiribati president did tell the American newspaper, the *Baltimore Sun*, in 2004, that Taiwan had promised his people 8 million US dollars over a four year period, mostly through projects such as upgrading an airport and possibly starting a fish-processing plant. The figure equates to about 90 dollars for each man, woman and child on Kiribati, far more than the one to two million US dollars which China previously had given in annual aid, the *Baltimore Sun* reported. And Kiribati certainly needs the money. An estimated 60 to 70 per cent of the islanders are jobless or severely underemployed, and the per capita annual income is less than 1,000 US dollars. As the *Baltimore Sun* reported, "Some on the outer islands live by subsistence fishing, but many migrate to the only developed island, crowded Tarawa, looking for jobs that don't exist."

China may try to come back to Kiribati, but would then have to come up with an offer that could beat the present aid packages from Taiwan. In the meantime, China is believed to be looking for a new site for a satellite tracking station near the Equator. The first possibility that was discussed was the Republic of Nauru, which has an equally favourable location. Nauru severed relations with Taipei in July 2002 and recognised Beijing. But then, in May 2005, Nauru re-established relations with Taiwan. Dollar diplomacy had paid off again.

But it is not certain that the loss of the Tarawa base was really that devastating for China. Some observers argue that the satellite dishes that China had at Tarawa were too small for monitoring US missile tests on Kwajalein. Des Ball, a professor at the Australian National University in Canberra and an expert on signals intelligence, told me that China's *Yuan Wang* tracking ships are far more useful for intelligence gathering: "These are packed with all sorts of communications gear." However, he also added that the loss of the Tarawa station was significant for another reason: it deprived Beijing of a land base in the Pacific, from where the movements and activities of the *Yuan Wang* ships could be coordinated.

Yuan Wang means "Long View" and is a fleet of maritime aerospace survey vessels, each with an impressive array of dishes and scanners. The creation of such a fleet was first proposed in 1965 by China's then Premier, Zhou Enlai, and, in 1968, Chairman Mao Zedong personally approved the plan. According to the website *Global Security*, which deals with military- and intelligence-related matters: "After passing through the storms of the Cultural Revolution, the *Yuen Wang* 1 and *Yuen Wang* 2 measuring ships were finally put into water on August 31, 1977 and September 1, 1978 respectively. This marked the end of the period in which China was unable to measure launch vehicle and satellite orbits from outside its national territory."

Since then, four more *Yuan Wang* ships have been added to the fleet. One of the tracking ships is permanently stationed in the Pacific while a second makes occasional visits. The rest sail around the Yellow Sea off the coast of China, along the Namibian coast in southern Africa, and in the Indian Ocean. To support these vessels, the Chinese Academy of Sciences also has a fleet of research ships sailing under the name *Xiang Yang Hong* ("the East is Red"), which can undertake additional upper-atmosphere missile and satellite research as well as hydrometeorology.

It may be argued that China has more legitimate security interests in the Pacific than any other ocean. Several of China's Western rivals have at various points in time carried out nuclear tests in the region. After World War II, the United States took over groups of islands whose colonial history began in the late 19th century with German domination. Germany was on the losing side of World War I, but Japan was then allied with Britain, France and the United States. The islands thus became a League of Nations mandate administered by Japan, but, in effect, Japanese colonies. Since Japan was on the other, losing side of World War II, it had to hand them over to the United Nations—which created the so-called "Trust Territory of the Pacific Islands," administered by the United States, again in reality as colonies.

It was not until the 1980s and 1990s that these islands became fully independent: the Republic of the Marshall Islands and the Federated States of Micronesia in 1986, and the Republic of Palau in 1994. The Northern Mariana Islands chose to remain a "commonwealth" in political union with the United States. The native population of the Marianas are Chamorros, the same as in nearby Guam, a US territory since 1898—but because the people of Guam suffered under Japanese occupation during World War II, and many Japanese-speaking Chamorros from the then Japan-administerd Marianas collaborated with the Japanese, there is little love lost between the two US territories and attempts to merge them have failed.

After signing the Trusteeship Agreement in 1947, the United States established a string of military bases on the newly acquired islands. Nuclear tests were carried out on Bikini and Enewetak in the Marshall Islands, followed by missile tests on Kwajalein. The nuclear tests actually began in 1946, when the islands were under US military occupation. The first was carried out on July 1 of that year, on Bikini—which prompted the French designer Louis Réard to name his design of a two-piece swimsuit for women after the atoll. The reasoning was that the burst of excitement created by it would be like a nuclear device.

Atmospheric nuclear tests on Bikini and Enewetak continued until 1962, and have caused serious health problems for the local population on those two atolls. On March 1, 1954, the United States detonated an extremely powerful hydrogen bomb, codenamed Castle Bravo, on Bikini. It was about 1,200 times stronger than the atomic bombs, which were dropped on Hiroshima and Nagasaki during World War II and generated radioactive fallout that killed a crew member of a Japanese fishing boat, the Daigo Fukuru Maru, and even contaminated the nearby Rongelap Atoll. Three days after the test, the inhabitants were evacuated to Kwajalein for examination and medical treatment.

Compensation for these nuclear tests became an issue when it was clear that many people near the sites suffered from thyroid disease, leukemia, hypertension and other radiation-related diseases. Bikini is still too contaminated to be inhabited; its local "government office" is located in the Marshall Islands capital of Majuro. In 1983, when it was clear that Marshall Islands was going to become independent, an agreement was reached with the United States. Washington promised to provide the Marshall Islands with 150 million US dollars as a settlement for the damages caused by the nuclear testing programme. That money was used to create a fund intended to generate 270 million US dollars for distribution over a 15-year period with average annual proceeds of approximately 18 million US dollars per year until 2001. These funds were to be distributed among the peoples of Bikini, Enewetak, Rongelap and Utrik, for medical and radiological monitoring, and the payment of claims. But the issue has yet to be settled as Marshall Islands has asked for more. In March 2009, Marshall Islands was renewing its appeal for two billion U.S. dollars in compensation from the United States government for damage caused by nuclear tests.

During my visit to the Marshall Islands in May 2004, I met and interviewed James Matayoshi, the mayor of Rongelap Atoll, in his office in Majuro. He pointed out that the people of Nevada and Utah, where the tests were moved to, in the 1960s, had received much higher compensation than the Marshall Islanders. Matayoshi told me that his mother, who was 16 in 1954, suffered from thyroid problems and hypertension. She also had two miscarriages before he was born. "For years, the United States claimed there was no problem, no contamination. But recently declassified documents show otherwise," Matayoshi said. He also indicated that local people were used as guinea pigs to study the effects of radiation. Why, he asked, were people evacuated when the first bomb was exploded on Bikini in 1946, and not when a much stronger device was detonated in 1954? The authorities knew where the winds were blowing, but they left inhabitants on the atolls for 72 hours before they were rescued.

China's official news agency *Xinhua* was quick to report the news about the renewed compensation claims in March 2009. That was perhaps for propaganda purposes, but China is also, for more strategic reasons, keeping a close eye on Kwajalein, even if it's being been done from the *Yuan Wang* ships rather than the old Tarawa satellite tracking station. Apart from serving as a support base for missile tests, Kwajalein, where a huge air field had been built, was also a vital link in the supply route for American forces during the Korean War in the early 1950s—a war also involving China, as hundreds of thousands of Chinese volunteers streamed down the Korean peninsula in support of the advance of the North Korean army.

Following the communist takeover in China and the subsequent war on the Korean peninsula, the United States

Central Intelligence Agency, the CIA, set up camp on Saipan in the Northern Marianas. Saipan is not big, only 22 kilometres long and eight kilometres wide, but the northern half of the island is mountainous and covered with dense, tropical forest. A secret intelligence headquarters called Capitol Hill was established on the top of one of the mountains, and became a covert training base for nationalist Chinese guerrillas from Taiwan, who were going to be sent to the mainland in a bid to re-conquer it from the communists. Some of these were the legendary "frogmen," divers who swam from smaller, Taiwan-held islands off the mainland and then went ashore to carry out sabotage and gather intelligence.

In the mid-1950s—already before the Dalai Lama fled to India in 1959—anti-Chinese Tibetan guerrillas were also trained on Saipan and then sent back to infiltrate a land very different from this tropical island. In the late 1950s, a small group of intelligence officers from Burma were also trained on Saipan. Later, they took part in Burmese government campaigns against the Communist Party of Burma, which was supported by China.

After the CIA abandoned the Saipan base in 1962, Capitol Hill became the headquarters of the Trust Territory. Today, it is where the government buildings for the Commonwealth of the Northern Mariana Islands are located—but it does not look like an ordinary capital, consisting mostly of barracks scattered on the top of a hill, far away from any other population centre on the island.

Kwajalein is now the only active US military installation in the former Trust Territory—but the United States has bigger naval and air bases on Guam and, of course, Hawaii. And the US Army Space and Strategic Defence Command administers Wake Island north of the Marshalls, a tiny atoll also with a huge airfield. Johnston Atoll east of Wake served in the 1990s as a disposal site for weapons, including chemical weapons.

Britain has also used islands in the Pacific for nuclear tests, but on a much smaller scale than the United States. Between 1957-58, Britain exploded thermonuclear weapons over Christmas Island—now called Kiritimati—and Malden Island in the Gilbert Islands, now Kiribati. And France carried out 193 nuclear tests, 40 of them atmospheric, on Moruroa and Fangatafua in French Polynesia between 1966 and 1996. In August 2006, an official report by the French government confirmed for the first time the link between an increase in the cases of thyroid cancer and France's atmospheric nuclear tests in the territory.

Past and present Western military activities in the Pacific dwarf China's once modest presence in Tarawa to insignificance. But there is nevertheless a cold war looming over the Pacific. China is indeed increasing its influence politically, economically and militarily—and the United States is beginning to take countermeasures. Continued protests against US bases in South Korea and Japan, and other frictions with the local population in those countries, have also prompted the Americans to look to its "own" islands in the Pacific as possible alternative places for military installations.

Guam, which is not far from the Asian mainland, is set to become the US military's main forward base in the Asia-Pacific region. According to Australian journalist Ben Bohane: "Washington has outlined plans for a 15 billion US dollar injection into Guam, relocating 8,000 Marines from Okinawa and their families, upgrades of existing air force and naval facilities, infrastructure for the island and a missile defence shield with crew...Between 40,000 and 60,000 people are expected to come to Guam in the years leading up to 2014 when completion of various military and civilian projects is expected on this Pacific fortress...soon this little island—'the aircraft carrier on land' or the 'USS Guam' as the Lieutenant Governor of Guam, Mike Cruz, half-jokes—is going to be seriously beefed up."

It has also been suggested that the old air base on Tinian in the Northern Marianas could be used again. Unlike Saipan, Tinian is completely flat. It was captured by the United States from the Japanese in July 1944, and the island was immediately transformed into the busiest airbase of the war. It was from Tinian that the planes carrying the atomic bombs "Little Boy" and "Fat Man" were launched against Hiroshima and Nagasaki in August 1945.

The airfields on Tinian are now overgrown and abandoned, but local politicians in the Northern Marianas have appealed to the US government to restore the old base to its former glory. That would provide a badly needed source of income for the territory, whose garment factories, with underpaid Chinese and other Asian workers, now have had to close as wages have been brought up to US standards. The Commonwealth of the Northern Marianas used to have 34 garment factories, all based on Saipan. They contributed around 60 million US dollars a year in direct taxes to the government. The last three garment factories were closed down on February 7, 2009.

The US Congressional Research Service stated in a 2007 report that the countries of the former Trust Territory— still very much dependent on the United States—"provide a vast buffer for Guam, which serves as the 'forward military bridgehead' from which to launch US operations along the Asia-Pacific security arc stretching from South Korea and Japan, through Thailand and the Philippines, to Australia. The US military is building up forces on Guam to help maintain deterrence and respond to possible security threats in the Pacific." During the Cold War, the report continued, the then Trust Territory "helped the United States to bolster its security posture in the Pacific, particularly in the 1980s... as the Soviet Union took steps to increase its presence in the region." Today, of course, the main concern is China.

Although the United States recognises the government in Beijing as the sole representative of China, it is obvious that Washington's interests in the Pacific are much closer to Taiwan's. Both the United States and Taiwan want to keep China out of the region. But China has made inroads even into the old Trust Territory. Chinese workers and migrants in the Northern Marianas and the Marshall Islands are only one aspect. While the Marshall Islands and Palau have diplomatic relations with Taiwan, the Federated States of Micronesia, FSM, recognises China. In return, China has showered FSM with loans and grants. China has also constructed a sports centre and government buildings in the FSM capital Kolonia— using, as elsewhere in the Pacific, Chinese rather than local workers. And, as elsewhere, large Chinese construction projects in FSM benefit the government in power rather than the local community. Bur China's main aim is to win over governments, not local populations.

Moreover, China maintains a large tuna fishing fleet in FSM, which also, along with the six other countries in the region with which China has diplomatic relations—Papua New Guinea, Vanuatu, Fiji, Tonga, Samoa and the Cook Islands—is an approved tourist destination for Chinese citizens. FSM was also included when Chinese Premier Wen Jiabao, in April 2006, held a summit in Fiji with members of the principal regional organisation, the Pacific Islands Forum. At the meeting, China and several Forum member states signed an agreement under which Wen pledged 375 million US dollars in aid and low interest loans as well as preferential tariffs for goods from the Pacific Islands, which recognised China.

Taiwan countered with its own Pacific summit. In September 2006, then Taiwanese president Chen Shui-bian travelled to Palau where he met representatives of the six countries in the region that recognise Taiwan: Kiribati, the Marshall Islands, Nauru, Palau, the Solomon Islands and Tuvalu. Agreements were signed on cooperative projects including law enforcement, tourism, public health, the environment, energy, agriculture and fisheries. On the way back to Taipei, Chen made a four-hour stopover in Guam where Raymond Burghardt, the chairman of the "American Institute in Taiwan—the unofficial US embassy in Taipei—greeted him. China was not pleased.

A second "Taiwan-Pacific Allies Summit" was held in Majuro, the Marshall Islands, in October 2007. The attendants were the same, and they reaffirmed "their commitments and support of Taiwan's right to be a member of the United Nations, World Health Organisation, and other international and regional organisations." A joke at the time was that global warming may deprive Taiwan of its Pacific allies; almost all of them are low-lying atolls which could disappear into the ocean if sea levels continue to rise.

But there seems to be little that Taiwan—and the United States—can do to stop China's advance into the Pacific. And, as the British Broadcasting Corporation, BBC, reported on August 14, 2007, "China's naval build-up has alerted American military officials to the previously unthinkable possibility that they might face competition in the Pacific Ocean, where the US has enjoyed naval dominance since World War II." The BBC quoted Richard Lawless, Deputy Undersecretary of Defence for Asia and Pacific Security Affairs, as saying that China's economic and political expansion into the Pacific "is the biggest shift in the region's power balance for more than 60 years." No Chinese warships have yet sailed into the Pacific Ocean, but submarines now frequently visit the region along with the *Yuan Wang* tracking ships.

Chinese intelligence activities in the Pacific region have also increased. In 2005, Chen Yonglin, a former first secretary at the Chinese consulate-general in Sydney who defected to Australia, claimed that Beijing had as many as 1,000 spies in that country alone. But his lawyers had told him to say no more for fear of jeopardizing his chances of receiving political asylum in Australia. The BBC reported at the time: "The cool response to Mr. Chen's and other defectors' requests say much about Western attitudes towards China. Whether in government, business or academic circles, there is a general reluctance to do or say anything that might upset Beijing and threaten access to its markets—not to mention its vast pool of high-paying and often highly gifted students."

The BBC went on to report that China has sent 600,000 students overseas in the past 25 years as part of a conscious policy of developing its science, technology and business skills. While the vast majority of them should not be suspected of being involved in any clandestine activities whatsoever— they belong to well-off families who simply want their children to get a good education—others are funded by the government and are expected to return to help their country. The BBC quoted Christian le Miere, Asia editor of *Jane's Country Risk*, a security publication, as saying that, "It's very easy for Chinese companies or intelligence agencies to approach these students—who are often quite nationalistic— and get them to collect information that might be of either commercial or military interest."

In April 2009, Australia was rattled by media reports that its new Prime Minister, Kevin Rudd, as well as other high ranking officials have become favourite targets for Chinese hackers. Various government and unnamed intelligence sources attributed the attacks to cyber-espionage efforts sponsored by the government in Beijing.

According to the daily *The Australian*, during his visit to China in August 2008, Prime Minister Rudd was targeted by hackers, who attempted to spy on his communications. All laptops and mobile phones used by the Australian delegation were said to have been attacked.

The Australian quoted several anonymous sources from inside the government and the intelligence agencies, who admitted that the threat of electronic espionage sponsored by the Chinese government is real and has been increasing in intensity for the past several years.

Speaking before the Australian Parliament on the issue of national security in December 2008, Rudd noted that "Australian policy, military and intelligence institutions, directions and capabilities are attractive intelligence targets for foreign powers... Electronic espionage in particular will be a growing vulnerability as the Australian Government and society become more dependent on integrated information technologies... Both commercial and state-based espionage, while not visible to the public eye, are inevitable." And China, naturally, is interested in Australia's vast mineral resources, and the role it plays in politics and defence in the southern hemisphere.

Rudd, a fluent Chinese speaker and former official at the Australian embassy in Beijing, is known to be a friend of Chinese culture and his premiership has helped build bridges between Australia's Asian and Caucasian communities. He was also the first Australian prime minister to publicly apologise to the country's indigenous population, the Aborigines, for the treatment that they had had to endure over more than a century of humiliating discrimination. The reports, therefore, were extremely damaging—for him personally and for ethnic harmony in Australia. *Reuters* reported on April 3, 2009: "Anti-Chinese sentiment has been building in Australia with opposition lawmakers accusing the Mandarin-speaking prime minister of being a 'roving ambassador' for China and too close to senior figures in Beijing."

Rudd, speaking in London after the G20 meeting of leading economies in April 2009, said he had not been advised of a specific attack, but the government was wary of electronic espionage. He also referred to his December 2008 speech, but was short on specifics about the alleged cyber attacks. But they appear to have taken place at a time Chinese companies were negotiating mining deals in Australia, which needed government approval.

Right-wing groups in the Asia-Pacific—and elsewhere— are warning that Western countries may one day regret allowing China to take advantage of their openness and tolerance. China, on its part, has indignantly denied the spying allegations, which it says stem from narrow-minded fears of legitimate commercial and industrial competition. And, in the wake of several spy scandals involving ethnic Chinese in the United States, an unfortunate wave of anti-Chinese sentiment has followed, from which even innocent students and migrants have suffered.

In nearby New Zealand, the daily *The Dominion Post* reported on June 12, 2005: "Two New Zealand groups championing people oppressed by the Chinese Government have claimed Chinese spies are active here and collecting intelligence on their activities. Auckland University security and intelligence expert Paul Buchanan has supported their claims, saying it was 'par for the course' that an emerging superpower such as China would spy on regional rivals Australia and New Zealand. But proof of espionage is almost impossible to find. The Government has indicated it will not question the Chinese embassy about the allegations, instead relying on its own methods—which remain top-secret—to detect spy activity."

In September 2007, the New Zealand government claimed that "foreign spies" had hacked into its computers. Their nationality was not mentioned, but the media, and the public, suspected they were Chinese. As in Australia, there was an unfortunate backlash against New Zealand's growing Asian population. New Zealand does not have the same deposits of mineral resources as Australia, but it is an important country when it comes to influence over the strategically important Pacific Ocean. China may also be concerned about the presence of Chinese dissidents in New Zealand, pro-democracy activists as well as members of the religious organisation Falun Gong, which is banned in China and seen there as a threat to national security because it has challenged the moral authority of the ruling communist party. On the other side of the Pacific, a top-secret study prepared in 1997 for the Royal Canadian Mounted Police and the Canadian Security Intelligence Service detailed an alleged pact between Chinese intelligence agencies, businessmen and criminal gangs operating in Canada. Codenamed "Sidewinder," the report was subsequently rewritten and given a new name, "Project Echo." The Canadian press accused the Canadian government of trying to water down the damning report so as not to upset relations between Canada and China. The original report specifically mentioned CITIC, or the China International Trust Investment Company, which is the largest Chinese company operating internationally. Among other Chinese companies mentioned in the "Sidewinder" report as part of the espionage network were the arms manufacturer Northern Industrial Corporation, or Norinco, and Poly Technologies. Smaller firms were also highlighted, such as film production companies which were "regularly in contact with prominent members of the Sun Yee On Triad."

The "Sidewinder" report became extremely controversial and was criticised by many as being "biased against China," and almost racist. But its basic findings received more credence when the US Federal Bureau of Investigations, FBI, in May 2001 arrested three Chinese-born scientists at the telecommunications giant Lucent Technologies and a smaller related enterprise in New Jersey. Accused of a "complicated scheme of corporate espionage," the three men were brought in handcuffs before a federal magistrate in Newark and detained without bail. They had allegedly stolen voice and data software from Lucent to set up a joint venture with a Beijing company that would become the Chinese equivalent of the US data-networking powerhouse Cisco Systems. The venture received 1.2 million US dollars in financing from Datang Telecom Technology, a Chinese-government controlled maker of communications equipment based in Beijing.

Rick Fisher, a China expert with the Jamestown Foundation in the United States, who served on the Republican

Policy Committee of the House of Representatives during a 1998 investigation of US technology transfers to China, described the arrests as "a signal that the United States needs to 'redouble' its efforts to find those persons working in this country for the benefit of the Chinese government." But was it just a joke that the China-financed New Jersey joint venture formed by the threesome was called Com Triad Technologies? Even if not part of a traditional Triad, the firm clearly saw itself as a high-tech version of China's age-old secret societies.

From the *Yuan Wang* tracking ships in the Pacific Ocean to Canada and corporate America, China's intelligence operations in the Asia-Pacific region have become more sophisticated. Peter Brookes, a senior fellow at the Heritage Foundation in the United States, quoted Sun Tzu, an ancient Chinese military strategist, in a May 31, 2005 article: "Sun Tzu said that intelligence is critical to success on the battlefield. It applies to the political and economic 'battlefield,' too. Accordingly, China is investing heavily in espionage to match its geopolitical aspirations."

Cook Islands-based New Zealand Pacific expert Ron Crocombe writes in his book *Asia in the Pacific Islands: Replacing the West*: "Asian spying may still be small compared with that of the USA, which has unmanned surveillance aircraft based in Guam as well as probably the most comprehensive system of submarine, telecommunications and land-based surveillance. But China is growing fast in this area."

China's access to intelligence gathered from Burmese naval bases in the Indian Ocean has sparked a similar rivalry in that region—and between Asia's two giants, China and India. In 1998, Indian intelligence recruited Burmese rebels to spy on the Burmese base on Coco Island in the Bay of Bengal, which had been upgraded with Chinese assistance. It was also suspected that Chinese personnel were assisting the Burmese in operating signals intelligence equipment on the island, and that India was a target.

The rebels, from the Karen and Arakanese ethnic minorities, were given the use of Landfall Island in the Andamans to keep arms and ammunition and as a safe haven after returning from their intelligence missions. But the entire operation was bungled by a colonel from India's military intelligence, who could have been paid off by the Burmese government. Several of the leaders of the Burmese rebels were killed and 34 others ended up in jail in Port Blair, the main town on the Andaman Islands. They were depicted in the Indian media as "pirates" and "gunrunners," but managed to get a sympathetic ear from a leading Indian human rights lawyer, Nandita Haksar. She describes in detail the arrangement the rebels from Burma had with the Indian authorities—and how it all went awfully wrong—in a book published in 2009, *Rogue Agent: How India's Military Intelligence Betrayed the Burmese Resistance.*

In 2005, Indian officials began to deny that there were "Chinese bases" in Burma, and to claim that there was no "listening post, radar or surveillance station belonging to the Chinese on Coco Island." But those statements missed the point that the bases and signals intelligence stations along Burma's coasts and on Coco Island were not Chinese-owned and run. They were—and are—Burmese bases which have benefitted from Chinese assistance. Burma and China have also signed agreements on intelligence sharing which cannot be ignored. And why would China not want to monitor the sea lanes through which it gets most of its oil supplies from the Middle East? They would be negligent, to say the least, if they did not keep a close eye on such a vital lifeline.

Most likely, India's turn-around in public was prompted by a desire not to offend the Burmese junta, which New Delhi also has been courting in order to lure it away from China's grip. This is just another example how the new Great Game is playing out in Burma, where China and India are jockeying for political influence and competing for access to the country's rich natural resources. And, as a political and economic rival, India would be foolish not to monitor China's activities in Burma. But perhaps some Karen and Arakanese rebels were not the best choice as human intelligence assets.

So the spying game continues, in the Pacific as well as the Indian Ocean. And, everywhere, China is the expanding, seemingly unstoppable power.

CHAPTER EIGHT
WHOSE PACIFIC CENTURY?

After the end of World War II, many people all over the world expected the 20th century to be the American Century. Western democracy had triumphed over the authoritarianism of Adolf Hitler's Nazi Germany, Benito Mussolini's Fascist Italy and Hideki Tojo's militaristic Japan. The Soviet Union had also been on the winning side of the war, but certainly did not become a model for anyone except fellow communists in some parts of the world. American pop culture swept the globe: blues, jazz and rock'n roll. The vast majority of people in all continents had a favourable image of the United States and what it stood for: freedom, democracy and a new, youthful way of life.

But many would argue that the American Century ended on November 22, 1963. On that day, US president John F. Kennedy, who had enjoyed worldwide popularity, was assassinated in Dallas, Texas, by a lone gunman. Under his successor, Lyndon B. Johnson, the war in Vietnam escalated, and millions of people all over the world took to the streets to demonstrate against "American imperialism." What remained of the American Century was buried on April 30, 1975—when North Vietnamese tanks crashed through the gates of the presidential palace in Saigon, ending the Vietnam war. The United States, a superpower, had been defeated by a small but stubborn country of peasants in Southeast Asia.

Then, of course, came the September 11, 2001 terror attacks in New York and Washington. The United States launched its disastrous "war on terror," which saw the world's most powerful democracy run torture chambers in Iraq, Afghanistan and at the Guantanamo base in Cuba. Tens of thousands of civilians were killed in Iraq and Afghanistan, as the United States bombarded suspected real or imagined terrorist strongholds. The rise of anti-Americanism across the world gave China a decided image advantage over the United States—and, after the collapse of the Soviet Union in 1989, China became the main challenge to the United States.

Despite its well-documented human rights abuses, China in the 1990s and early 2000s came to be seen by an increasing number of people, especially in the Asia-Pacific region but also across the globe, as a more benign power than the United States—even in countries that had been close American allies for decades. A 2005 Australian survey by the Lowy Institute, a Sydney-based private think-tank, shocked Washington. Barely half of the respondents in Australia had positive feelings about the United States. Joshua Kurlantzick, an American author who has studied the rise of China, writes in his book *Charm Offensive: How China's Soft Power Is Transforming the World*: "Worse, 57 per cent of Australians thought that America's foreign policies were a potential threat—equivalent to the percentage of Australians worried about the rise of Islamic fundamentalism. This despite the fact that in 2002 a massive bomb in Bali, Indonesia, allegedly planted by radical Islamists, killed more than two hundred people, most of them Australians."

In the same Lowy Institute poll, nearly 70 per cent of Australians viewed China positively. According to Kurlantzick: "Lest anyone think that was an aberration, another study showed that more than 50 per cent of Australians supported a proposed free trade agreement with China, while only 34 per cent supported such a pact with the United States." China has managed to alter its image abroad from that of threat to opportunity, from danger to benefactor.

This, Kurlantzick argues, has been achieved through a concept called "soft power," or leading by example and attracting others to do what you want. China, rather than Japan, is emerging as the main economic and political superpower in the Asia-Pacific region, mainly because Japan has failed to cultivate soft power. Tokyo seems to believe that aid and investment is enough to win influence, while China is cultivating a more proactive foreign policy. Moreover, with only a small diaspora in the developing world, Japan has been unable to undertake the kind of outreach to overseas compatriots that Beijing can do with new and old overseas Chinese communities.

When China in the 1970s supported the communist insurgency in Thailand, it was seen by the establishment in Bangkok as an enemy. Sino-Thai businessmen in those times downplayed their Chinese ancestry so as not to be perceived as a fifth column for China's designs for the region. Today, as Kurlantzick writes, even "Thai politicians tout their Chinese background, partly because it seems popular with the public that views Beijing as cool, rich and attractive." Mainland China, not Taiwan, is today considered the motherland of Thailand's millions of businessmen of Chinese descent.

In 1997, during the Asian financial crisis, China won praise in the region when it refrained from devaluing its currency, which helped stabilise the region's economy. China has also become an increasingly active player in multilateral organisations that include Southeast Asian states such as the Association of Southeast Asian Nations, or ASEAN, and the East Asia Summit, which includes China, Japan, South Korea, India, Australia and New Zealand. China's aid to the region is growing, as was, at least until the financial meltdown, Chinese tourism. Investment in Cambodia, Laos and Burma has slowed down somewhat but is still significant. In July 2005, a congressional panel in Washington concluded that China aims to displace the United Sates in Southeast Asia. A participant argued that, "US ties with Southeast Asia suffered from perceptions that America 'has no discernible policy for Southeast Asia beyond counterterrorism'."

The rise of China—and Chinese migration—is also likely to upset economic and demographic balances in vulnerable areas like the Russian Far East, the Pacific islands, and parts of Southeast Asia such as northern Burma, Laos and Cambodia. This movement is indeed unstoppable partly because of population pressure inside China—and the Chinese government's policy of encouraging migration because the new Chinese diaspora plays a vital part in China's aspirations to become a great power. In the long term, this could lead to problems of different natures, despite the policy of "soft power." For Russia, it could mean the "loss", in reality if not in name, of its huge Far Eastern Federal District.

For the United States, it is inevitable that a clash of interests is going to take place in the Pacific Ocean, with China likely to overtake Japan as the leading economic power in the Asia-Pacific region within the next few decades. Chinese migration and the role of Chinese diasporas in the region are issues that warrant careful study. It may not be a deliberate deployment of a "fifth column," but, as Hungarian sinologist Nyiri Pal points out, "a case of local political will and migratory *fait accompli*, of which Beijing is simply taking advantage."

But the tables may turn as the United States is bouncing back. Barack Obama's victory in the November 2008 presidential election has once again altered the United States' image abroad—and this time, from Washington's point of view, in a very positive direction. I was in the Cambodian capital Phnom Penh when the election result was announced and there was jubilation in the streets. In Indonesia—where no more than ten per cent of the population had a favourable view of the United States when Bush was in the White House—Obama is extremely popular. Obama lived in Indonesia as a child, from 1967 to 1971, with his mother and stepfather, and attended school in Jakarta. In Obama's father's home village in Kenya, people danced, played drums and waved American flags. Obama is also the most popular United States president among Europeans since Kennedy.

Obama's administration is far more willing than that of his predecessor, George W. Bush, to listen to the rest of the world rather than ordering it around, so even the United States is beginning to employ some "soft power" in its foreign policy. Obama has reached out to old foes such as Iran, relaxed restrictions on money transfers to Cuba, and even sent a delegate to talk to the junta in Burma. On March 24, 2009, Stephen Blake, director of Southeast Asian Affairs at the State Department, visited the new capital Naypyidaw and held talks with Nyan Win, Burma's foreign minister. The United States is not likely to condone human rights abuses by the Burmese generals more than Bush did, but Washington seems to have realised that its policy thus far has had no effect other than driving Burma into the arms of the Chinese.

As China gets more powerful and spreads its influence all over the world, it is also likely that hitherto relatively positive perceptions may change. Anti-Chinese riots in the Solomon Islands and Tonga may serve as harbingers of what China could be expecting to happen in other countries in the Asia-Pacific region, when its influence there reaches a similar breaking point. There were also serious anti-Chinese riots in the Indonesian capital Jakarta at the height of the 1997-1998 economic crisis, although those were directed against the city's old Chinese mercantile class, not at newly arrived migrants.

A December 2007 survey by the US-based Pew Research Centre found that, "while global opinion of China remains mostly positive, it has soured in recent years—although not as widely as have attitudes toward the United States. In nine of 15 countries for which trend data is available, the proportion of the public saying it views China favourably has shrunk over the past two years. The largest declines are observed among China's Asian neighbours (Japan, South Korea, and India), but significant slippage is also seen in Western Europe (Britain, France, Germany, Spain.)"

In some countries in the Asia-Pacific, the more sordid sides of China's global reach—human smuggling and organised crime—have contributed to negative perceptions of Chinese in general, and that not only on some remote Pacific islands. Japan is one example. Small Chinese communities have been living in Yokohama, Kobe and other port cities for generations. The first Chinese to settle in Japan were petty traders, mostly Cantonese, who arrived in the 19th century. Yokohama's Chinatown was founded in 1873, complete with Chinese restaurants, a school and a temple. The community in Kobe consisted mostly of migrants from Jiangsu and Zhejiang. But wars between China and Japan in the early and mid 20th century led to a sharp decline in the number of Chinese living on the Japanese islands. Then, with Japan's expansion during the years leading up to World War II—and during the war— more Chinese settled in Japan.

Most of them came from Taiwan, which was a Japanese colony from 1895 to the end of World War II, when it was handed back to China—at that time, the Kuomintang-ruled Republic of China. In 1940, official statistics showed that 20,284 out of 22,499 Chinese living in Japan came from Taiwan. When the communists took over the mainland in 1949, and Taiwan, and a few other, smaller islands, were all that remained of the Republic of China, many Taiwanese chose to remain in Japan. Unlike the Koreans, who emerged bitterly anti-Japanese from the colonial experience, the Taiwanese—both on the island and those who settled in Japan—have remained much more pro-Japanese.

Korea was an ancient kingdom that was brutally occupied and absorbed by Japan in the early 20th century. Taiwan, on the other hand, was a lawless, neglected Chinese province, and the Japanese, having taken it over in 1895, modernised the island, improved the infrastructure and built schools and hospitals. The fact that Taiwan was ruled from the mainland for only four years since 1895—from 1945, when it was reunited with the mainland, till the communist takeover of the mainland, and the retreat to the island of the Kuomintang government, in 1949—has contributed to its strong feeling of being a separate nation and not necessarily part of a worldwide Chinese fraternity loyal to Beijing.

Until the 1980s, there was little love lost between the Mandarin-speaking mainlanders who had retreated to Taiwan in 1949 and the native Taiwanese they ruled, who speak a Fujianese dialect. While the ruling Kuomintang dreamt of re-conquering the mainland under the banner of the Republic of China, the Taiwanese had no such desire. And, with the democratisation of Taiwan in the late 1980s and early 1990s, even the Kuomintang began to focus on issues concerning the island rather than the mainland. Today, there is little or no desire on the part of any group of people in Taiwan to follow the example of Hong Kong and Macau and become a "special administrative region" of the People's Republic of China. Although Tokyo recognises the People's Republic, a special relationship has always existed between Japan and Taiwan. The first Taiwan-born Kuomintang president, Lee Teng-hui, a Hakka who served from 1988 and 2000, was partly educated in Japan, speaks fluent Japanese, and has never been to the mainland.

But then, in the 1980s, a new wave of Chinese migrants began to arrive in Japan. When Beijing in 1979 began to approve overseas travel by Chinese citizens—and the then government of prime minister Yasuhiro Nakasone, at about the same time, announced a scheme aimed at raising the number of overseas students in Japanese universities to 100,000—many Chinese applied. In fact, more than 30 per cent of those who were granted such visas came from China, and the official number of Chinese students in Japan increased to 22,810 in 1998 from, only 23 in 1978. It is anybody's guess how many of them actually were students, but it led to a rapid expansion of the Chinese community in Japan. In 1998, it was estimated that 230,000 Chinese were residing legally in Japan, while illegals—including "visitors", "students" with expired visas and immigrants smuggled into the country—numbered at least 70,000. By 2002, Chinese who had entered Japan legally numbered 527,000, while snakeheads continued to bring in a huge but unknown number of illegals by boat and other means. Incidents of theft, extortion, robbery, abduction and murder by members of new crime syndicates became endemic in Japan's previously peaceful Chinese communities.

Rivalries between gangsters from Beijing, Fujian and Shanghai have erupted into shoot-outs in Tokyo's main entertainment district, Kabuki-cho in Shinjuku, and in other places in Japan as well. Guns are smuggled in from China and from Russia across the Japan Sea. Several clubs in Kabuki-cho now also show a new type of "hostess" on photo displays outside their well-guarded entrances: blondes from Russia, Ukraine and Belarus. But the bouncers at the doors are now mostly Chinese. During a visit to Kabuki-cho, Nicholas Kristoff, a correspondent for the *New York Times*, met a member of Japan's traditional organised crime gangs, the *yakuza*, who told him that, "Our biggest problem is the rise of the Chinese mafia. The Chinese gangs are taking business from us in every area—in prostitution, in gambling, in fencing stolen goods." While it is true that Japan's own crime gangs have become more violent in recent years, the Chinese gangs are even more ruthless—which has led to strong, anti-Chinese sentiments among many ordinary Japanese.

The Pew Research Centre's survey shows that, in 2007, only 29 per cent of Japanese respondents had a favourable view of China—down from 55 per cent in 2002. In the Asia-

Pacific region, there is also a downward trend also in South Korea, although not as sharp as in Japan: in 2007, 52 per cent viewed China favourably, compared with 66 per cent in 2002. 89 per cent of the South Koreans considered China's growing military power a threat—which is hardly surprising, given that China is a close ally of the communist-ruled North Korea, the South's rival and traditional enemy.

Korea is often described as East Asia's ethnically most homogenous country, but it does have a Chinese minority as well—and there is an old Chinatown in the Myongdong shopping area in downtown Seoul, with Chinese restaurants, Chinese herbal medicine stores, and a Chinese school. In ancient times, Korea was a fiercely independent kingdom, but it has to pay tribute to the Chinese emperor. But by the terms of the Treaty of Shimonoseki in 1895, which ended the first main war between China and Japan, China not only had to cede Taiwan to Japan—but also give all its claims to independent Korea. No more tribute was to be paid to the Chinese Emperor, and the peninsula came under Japanese domination, which at that time was spreading rapidly in East Asia.

Chinese migration to Korea probably began as early as the 13th century, but it was not until the 1880s that as mass movement began. The Chinese Qing Dynasty sent some 3,000 soldiers to Korea, and they were followed by a group of 40 Chinese merchants. In 1882, the Chinese and Korean governments concluded a trade treaty, allowing merchants from China to engage in various kinds of businesses in Korea. According to Park Kyung-tae a researcher at Sungkonghoe University, "at the end of the 19th century there were several natural disasters in Shandong province, China," prompting even more Chinese to move to Korea.

Korea became officially a Japanese possession in 1910, and by then many Chinese had settled in Seoul as well as in several port cities, among them Incheon, where they ran restaurants, sundry goods stores, medicine shops and traditional, underground Chinese-style banks. Chinese migration to Korea increased during the first decades of Japanese rule. Although constrained by Japanese regulations, many Chinese labourers and merchants moved from the chaos of China, then a fragmented nation ruled by warlords, to the relative stability of Japanese-occupied Korea.

Thus, the Chinese population in Korea grew from around 10,000 in 1910 to nearly 70,000 in the early 1930s. But one incident caused their numbers to decrease. In July 1931, a row erupted over a waterway being dug with Korean labour on the other side of the border, where the Japanese were busy taking over Manchuria, which, in 1932, became the puppet state of Manchukuo with the last Emperor of China, Pu Yi, as it head of state. But, in reality, it also become a Japanese colony. While this transition was in progress, there were reports that Chinese farmers and police had attacked and wounded Korean workers at Wanbaoshan across the border. However, scholars argue, the Koreans were unaware that these stories were based on a distortion by Japanese-owned newspapers. Thousands of Koreans in Incheon, Pyongyang and Seoul took to the streets chanting "Death to the Chinese!"

It was the first documented racial riot in modern Korean history, which left about 142 Chinese dead, 546 seriously injured, and hundreds of Chinese shops and properties torched and looted. At least a thousand Chinese fled back to China by ship from Incheon, while 16,800 sought safety at the Chinese consulate in Seoul. Numbers began to fall even further when another full-scale war broke out between China and Japan in 1937. After World War II, more Chinese returned to China. By the late 1950s, only 15,000 Chinese remained in the northern part of the then divided Korea, most of them making a living as market gardeners. In the south, there were about 22,000 Chinese, and, due to the discrimination they suffered under the ultra-nationalistic regimes of Syngman Rhee from 1948 to 1960, and Park Chung Hee from 1961 to 1979, many re-migrated to the United States, Canada, Australia and Brazil.

But a few thousand remained in Myong-dong, where the Chinese embassy also used to be located. Until August 1992, it was the embassy of the Republic of China, not, as today, that of the People's Republic. The local headquarters of the Kuomintang is located in the same lane in Myong-dong, only a few hundred meters from the old embassy that Taiwan once controlled. In the old days—when Taiwan and South Korea were close and staunch anti-communist allies—

that was hardly surprising. But, for years, the embassy of the People's Republic of China and the Kuomintang headquarters were neighbours by accidents of history. Now, the Chinese have moved to another, more modern building in another part of Seoul.

While many Chinese have maintained their customs and family traditions, and still speak Chinese at home, they are not a vocal or visible community as elsewhere in Asia. Intermarriages have also taken place between Koreans and ethnic Chinese in the country. In the 1990s, out of 1,100 students at the Overseas Chinese School in the Yonhi-dong district, 300 had Korean mothers. The Chinese in South Korea are fairly well assimilated and rather than running restaurants and stores, a younger generation of Chinese have become doctors, engineers, architects and even entertainers; one of South Korea's most popular female singers, Jang Ri-in, is a actually a Chinese born in the southern province of Sichuan. Her Chinese name is Zhang Liyin and she did not move to Korea until 2003, at the age of 14. Her rhythm and blues voice has made her a celebrity in her new homeland.

Jang Ri-in is perhaps an exception as she entered Korea as a student of music and dance, and later became a local star. But as the South Korean economy grew in the 1980s and 1990s, more unskilled workers were also needed. In 2000, there were as many as 260,000 foreign workers in South Korea, and of those 165,000 were unauthorised migrants. The largest groups were the Chinese, 85,429, including ethnic Koreans from China, followed by Bangladeshis, Mongolians, Filipinos, Thais, Pakistanis and Uzbeks. A new Chinatown emerged in Sillim-dong and Bongchon-dong areas in the southern parts of Seoul, which were quickly becoming small enclaves of Chinese culture. Stores and supermarkets displayed signs and billboards in Chinese characters. Most of the male residents work as construction laborers or factory workers, while women have found jobs in restaurants.

For entirely different reasons, attempts have also been made to restore the old Chinatown in Incheon. During the Japanese time, it had a population of more than 10,000 inhabitants and was crowded with hundreds of Chinese restaurants, medicine stores and even a Chinese church. Most Chinese left after World War II and the establishment of a communist regime in Beijing, when restrictions were imposed on trade with China. Park Chung Hee's ultranationalist policies forced even more Chinese to emigrate to the West. Although most Chinese had left by the late 1970s, near the town's subway station, a distinctive, 11-metre high gate remained, marking the entrance to the old Chinatown and reminding visitors of what once had been a thriving commercial community in this Korean port city. Then, in 2002, to capitalise on the large number of Mainland Chinese visitors to South Korea, the Incheon city council planned to revive its Chinatown at a cost of 6.2 million US dollars. Not much has happened on that score, and Incheon's Chinatown has remained a tourist attraction, not a destination for Chinese migration.

By August 2007, the number of foreign workers in South Korea was over a million of whom 210,000 were unauthorized—and most of them had settled in and around Seoul. As a per cent of the population, that is a much higher figure than in Japan. But, as in Japan, many xenophobic citizens tend to blame escalated violent crime on the influx of "outsiders." As the worldwide economic meltdown, which began in 2008, is likely to worsen, attitudes towards "foreigners"—and their respective home countries— may also become more hostile.

Even in Africa, where China had become a dominant economic power, attitudes began to change following the economic meltdown. Lydia Polgreen wrote in the *New York Times* of March 26, 2009: "With a no-strings-attached approach and a strong appetite for risk, China seemed to offer Africa a complete economic and political alternative to the heavily conditioned aid and economic restructuring that Western countries and international aid agencies pressed on Africa for years, often with uninspiring consequences. Rising China, seeking friends and resources, seemed to be issuing blank cheques."

Today, China's thirst for commodities may remain the same, but, Polgreen continues, state-owned Chinese companies are "bargain-hunting for copper and iron in more stable places like Zambia and Liberia... Chinese companies are now driving harder bargains and avoiding some of the most chaotic corners of the continent." For years, China was also importing huge quantities of timber from Africa, but that has slowed down—which was welcomed by environmentalists who were witnessing the destruction of crucial wildlife habitats. Now, perhaps the chimpanzees and gorillas will be saved.

But regardless of some setbacks and negative trends in recent years, China is, and will remain, an economic power that the rest of the world cannot ignore. On a visit to Beijing in April 2009, Venezuela's outspoken president, Hugo Chavez, told his Chinese counterpart: "No one can be ignorant that the centre of gravity has moved to Beijing. During the financial crisis, China's actions have been highly positive for the world. Currently, China is the biggest motor driving the world amidst this crisis of international capitalism."

Critics may argue that Chavez is known for his anti-Americanism, and, after all, he was in Beijing to negotiate ways of boosting Venezuelan oil exports to China. But after the previous Cold War, when the United States was pitted against the Soviet Union, a new bipolar world is indeed emerging with the United States and China as the main superpowers—and rivals, even if the official rhetoric is filled with talks about friendship and cooperation. And China will continue to rise in certain parts of the world. In the Russian Far East, China has no rival. In Southeast Asia, China is becoming at least as powerful as the United States, and Chinese migration to Burma, Laos and Cambodia is bound to alter the demographics of parts of those countries. Not only Chinese migration but also Chinese political and military influence are bound to alter many aspects of life and society in the Asia-Pacific region. Chinese cultural influence is also increasing as Chinese music and film—and now not only from Hong Kong and Taiwan—are gaining popularity in many Asian countries. China, after all, is an Asian country—unlike the United States, which to many Asians is still remote, alien and often perceived as threatening to local values, customs and traditions.

At the dawn of the 21st century, China's southward expansion, which began centuries ago, has gained a new momentum, which no financial crisis can stop or reverse.

Chinese migration, and the worldwide web that is connected with it, is bound to change the map of the world. China's influence in Southeast Asia is solid, and based not only on recent migration but, more importantly, on the centuries-old, so called "bamboo network"—inter-connected, economically powerful Chinese communities in all countries in Southeast Asia. With mainland China's transition from socialism to capitalism, Southeast Asia's expatriate Chinese entrepreneurs have contributed greatly to the China's becoming a new economic superpower in the region.

The Chinese communities in Thailand, Malaysia, Indonesia, Singapore and even the Philippines may remain exactly that: local financial powerhouses with links to China. The head of one of Thailand's biggest Sino-Thai conglomerates, Charoen Pokhband, even advises the Thai government on its relations with China, and is known to have helped the Chinese government with its lobbying efforts in Thailand and elsewhere. Northern Burma, Laos and Cambodia, on the other hand, have become more integral parts of China's network, as it is expanding its influence in all respects into the Great Golden Peninsula: economically, politically, and with a massive influx of migrants.

The United States seems to have "ceded" Southeast Asia to China's sphere of influence. Robert Sutter, a visiting professor of Asian affairs at Georgetown University, wrote in February 2005: "The loss of US ability to revert a containment policy of pressure against China seems small. In the past, Asian countries were unlikely to side with the United States against China out of concern that China might react aggressively; now the Asian governments are loathe to do so for fear of jeopardising positive benefits they receive from China. In either case, the net effect is that it has long been true that a US containment policy against China would not win much support in Asia. Since Asian countries have long been reluctant to choose between the United States and China, it would be foolish for US policy to react to China's rise by trying to compete directly with China for influence in the region."

It is in the Pacific that the main competition between the United States and China will take place—a rivalry that could lead to conflict, as it is the buffer between the two superpowers where both have what they consider legitimate security interests. This was emphasised by US president Barack Obama in a speech before the Australian parliament in November 2011: "Our enduring interests in the region demand our enduring presence in this region. The United States is a Pacific power, and we are here to stay." At the same time, Obama announced an agreement with Australia that will expand military cooperation between the long-time allies and boost America's presence in the region.

The small Pacific island countries may soon find themselves pieces in a much bigger game that increases their strategic significance even more. Tonga, the Cook Islands, Samoa, Vanuatu, Papua New Guinea and the Federated States of Micronesia are already within China's expanding sphere of influence—and the question is not only what Taiwan, but especially the United States, is going to do to counter this seemingly irreversible development. Other Pacific countries may soon also follow suit as Chinese pressure, coupled with promises of aid and generous loans, becomes even more intense.

The 21st century is bound to be not the American Century but the Pacific Century. The question is only *whose* Pacific Century?

NOTES ON COUNTRIES
AND TERRITORIES

The Far Eastern Federal District (Russia)

The largest, and most sparsely populated, of Russia's eight federal districts. Land area 6,215,900 square kilometres and 6.5 million people, or a density of only 1.1 inhabitant per square kilometre. Administrative centre: Khabarovsk. The area is rich in oil and natural gas, timber and minerals, including gold.

Papua New Guinea

The eastern half of Papua New Guinea was divided between Germany and Britain until World War One, then by Australia until independence in 1975.

The British Queen is the head of state, represented by a local governor-general. The largest and most populous country in the Pacific; 462,840 square kilometres and 6.7 million people. Capital: Port Moresby. Papua New Guinea is underdeveloped but is rich in mineral resources, including oil, copper and gold. It is also densely forested.

The Solomon Islands

A former British protectorate in Melanesia which became independent in 1978. It consists of nearly 1,000 islands, altogether 28,400 square kilometres, with 530,000 inhabitants. Vast resources of timber and other forest products; some gold on the island of Guadalcanal. Recognises the Republic of China (Taiwan). Capital: Honiara. The British Queen is the head of state, represented by a local governor-general.

Vanuatu

Formerly known as the New Hebrides, this group of Melanesian islands was administered jointly by Britain and France until independence in 1980, when it became the

Republic of Vanuatu. Area 12,190 square kilométres and 245,000 inhabitants. Capital: Port Vila. The islands survive on tourism, plantation agriculture, cattle raising—and Vanuatu's status as a tax haven and offshore financial centre.

Fiji
Fiji, which was a British colony until 1970, is one of the most prosperous countries in the South Pacific. Tourism and sugar exports are major sources in income. Area 18,274 square kilometres and 850,000 inhabitants, of whom nearly half are descendants of labourers the British brought in from India. Capital: Suva. A republic since 1987.

Tonga
The only kingdom in the South Pacific. Comprised of 176 islands scattered over 700,000 square kilometres of ocean. Fifty-two of the islands are inhabited by approximately 100,000 people of whom nearly a quarter live in the capital, Nuku'alofa. Tonga was a British-protected state from 1900 to 1970, then fully independent. A major source of income is remittances from Tongans working abroad, mainly in New Zealand, Australia and the United States. Most inhabitants are subsistence farmers, or fishermen.

Samoa
Neither a republic nor a hereditary kingdom, Samoa's head of state is a traditional chief. The western Samoan islands were German from the turn of last century to World War One, when New Zealand took over. Samoa became independent in 1962. Area 2,831 square kilometres, 180,000 inhabitants. Capital: Apia. Most people are subsistence farmers, or live on remittances from relatives working in New Zealand and other countries.

American Samoa
A US "unincorporated territory" since the turn of the last century. Area 199 square kilometres, 66,000 inhabitants. Capital: Pago Pago. Most people work in tuna canneries, and for the US government, including the military.

Cook Islands
A total of 240 square kilometres of land—and 1,800,000 square kilometres of ocean. Population: not more than 20,000, and at least that many Cook Islanders live in New Zealand. All Cook Islanders are citizens of New Zealand, which is responsible for defence and foreign relations. Capital: Avarua on the main island, Rarotonga.

French Polynesia
A French possession since 1889, now an "Overseas Territory" of France. Area 4,167 square kilometres, 267,000 inhabitants. Capital: Papeete. French Polynesia has a higher living standard than any independent Pacific nation. The economy is based mainly on subsidies from France, tourism, black pearls—and the popular health drink *noni*.

Tuvalu
The smallest of the Polynesian states, consisting of four reef islands and five atolls totalling 26 square kilometres and 10,000 inhabitants. The islands, then known as the Ellice Islands, were British until 1978. British Queen remains head of state, represented by a local governor-general. Tuvalu, which lacks natural resources, recognises the Republic of China (Taiwan), which provides it with generous development assistance.

Kiribati
Comprised of 32 atolls and one raised island—811 square kilometres of land and 3.5 million square kilometres of ocean. Formerly a British colony, it has been an independent republic since 1979. Kiribati is classified as one of the world's poorest countries; its exports consist almost solely of copra and fish. Recognises the Republic of China (Taiwan), which, in turn, provides Kiribati with aid.

Nauru
A former German colony, it was administered by Britain, Australia and New Zealand until it became an independent republic in 1968. With its 21 square kilometres of land and less than 10,000 people, it is the world's smallest republic. It used to be rich from phosphate mining, but now survives as

a tax haven and "financial centre". Recognises the Republic of China (Taiwan).

The Republic of the Marshall Islands (RMI)

A German colony prior to World War One, then under Japanese rule until World War Two, when it was occupied by the United States. An independent republic since 1986; 181 square kilometres and 62,000 inhabitants. Sells fishing rights to other countries, and recognises the Republic of China (Taiwan). Capital: Majuro, where most people live.

Federated States of Micronesia

A federation of four island states. Like the Marshall Islands and Palau, it was a German colony prior to World War One, then under Japanese rule until World War Two, when it was occupied by the United States. Independent in 1986. Consists of 702 square kilometres with 110,000 inhabitants. Palikir on the island of Pohnpei serves as the administrative centre. Maintains close relations with the People's Republic of China.

Palau

First a German colony, then, after World War One, a Japanese possession, and, after World War Two administered by the United States. Became an independent republic in 1994. 459 square kilometres and 20,000 inhabitants. One of six Pacific states that recognise the Republic of China (Taiwan).

Guam

An "unincorporated" US territory since 1898, before which it was a Spanish colony. Comprised of 541 square kilometres with 178,000 inhabitants. Tourism—mainly from Japan and South Korea—is a major source of income. Twenty-nine per cent of Guam is administered by the US military, which maintains several military installations on the island.

Commonwealth of the Northern Mariana Islands (CNMI)

Now a commonwealth in political union with the United States, the Northern Marianas were Spanish until 1898, then Germany ruled them until 1919, when the Japanese took over. They came under United States rule at the end of World War

Two. Area 462 square kilometres, 87,000 inhabitants. Tourism to the main island of Saipan—mostly Japanese—is a major source of income besides subsidies from the United States.

Burma
Now officially known as Myanmar, Burma has been an independent republic since 1948. Prior to that it was a British colony. The country has been under severe military rule since 1962. Area 676,000 square kilometres, 60 million inhabitants. The country is rich in mineral resources, including precious stones, oil and natural gas, but decades of mismanagement by the military has left the economy in a shambles. Capital since 2005: Naypyidaw; main city: Rangoon (Yangon).

Thailand
An ancient kingdom, Thailand was never colonised by any Western power. Area 513,120 square kilometres, 66 million inhabitants. Capital: Bangkok. Thailand has the highest living standard in Southeast Asia after Malaysia, Singapore and Brunei. The economy is strong and based on manufacturing, agriculture, and tourism.

Laos
A former French protectorate and, after 1954, an independent kingdom, Laos has been under communist rule since December 1975. With 236,800 square kilometres and 6.8 million inhabitants, it is the least densely populated country in Southeast Asia. Capital: Vientiane. In recent years, Laos has received significant investments from Thailand, Vietnam and, above all, China. Still poor, the country nevertheless has an enormous hydroelectric power potential.

Cambodia
A former French protectorate like Laos, it became an independent kingdom in 1953. The country was devastated during the wars in Indochina in the 1960s and, especially, the 1970s. For many years under communist rule, the monarchy was restored in 1993. 181,035 square kilometres, 14.8 million people. Capital: Phnom Penh. The country receives massive investments—and aid—from China.

NOTES ON SOURCES

Introduction and Acknowledgements

The quotes from Nyiri Pal and Igor Savielev (including the excerpt from the 1995 Shanghai New Migrants Research Project) come from *Globalizing Chinese Migration: Trends in Europe and Asia* (Aldershot: Ashgate Publishing, 2002.) I also attended the conference on Chinese migration in Budapest on May 26-27, 2000 and submitted a paper on "Illegal Aliens Smuggling to and through Southeast Asia's Golden Triangle," which is included in the volume.

The quote from William H. Myers is from his essay "Of Qinqing, Qinshu, Guanxi, and Shetou: The Dynamic Elements of Chinese Irregular Population Movement" in Paul J. Smith, *Human Smuggling: Chinese Migrant Trafficking and the Challenge to America's Immigration Tradition* (Washington: the Centre for Strategic & International Studies, 1997.)

The rest of the chapter is based on my own research; see, for instance, my paper "Diasporas in China's Security Strategy" in Robert G. Wirsing and Rouben Azizian (eds.) *Ethnic Diasporas & Great Power Strategies in Asia.* (Honolulu, Hawaii and New Delhi: India Research Press and the Asia-Pacific Center for Security Studies, 2007.) I also attended that conference in Honolulu on October 12-14, 2004.

Chapter One

In the Russian Far East in April, May and June 2006, I interviewed Gennady Ivanovich Shishkin of the *Itar-Tass* News Agency in Vladivostok; Alexander Sukharenko and Vitaly Nomokonov at the Centre for the Study of Organised Crime at the Far Eastern State University's Law Institute in Vladivostok; Lyudmila Erokhina at the Vladivostok State University of Economics and Services in Vladivostok; Sergei

G. Pushkarev, president of the Foundation for Migration Policy in Northeast Asia; Viktor Larin at the Russian Academy of Sciences, Far Eastern Branch, Vladivostok; Luidmila Ivanovna Gallyamova also at the Russian Academy of Sciences, Far Eastern Branch, Vladivostok; "Evgeniyi," an immigration officer in Khabarovsk who requested anonymity; Andrey Zabiyako at the Amur State University in Blagoveshchensk.

The excerpt from the book by Yuri Ufimtsev (*KGB v KHP: Skvoz Bambukovyi Zanaves*, or "KGB in China: A Peek Through the Bamboo Curtain") and other Russian documents were translated by Evgeniyi Belenky. I also visited the Xianggang restaurant in Khabarovsk and talked to the owner, Natasha, as well as guests in the restaurants and Chinese traders in the Chinese markets in Khabarovsk and Blagoveshchensk.

I also used information provided in Viktor Dyatlov (ed.) *A Bridge Across the Amur River: International Migration and Migrants in Siberia and the Far East* (in Russian and English, The Natalis Publishing House, Irkutsk.)

See also "Economic Security and Chinese Migration to the Russian Far East" by Elizabeth Wishnick; "Chinese Migration to Russia: Road to Conflict or Harmony?" by Vladimir Portyakov; "Managing the Ethno-Strategic Security Implications of Russia's Demographic Crisis" by Graeme P. Herd; "Diasporas in Russia's Security Strategy" by Igor Zevelev in "Diasporas in China's Security Strategy" in Robert G. Wirsing and Rouben Azizian (eds.) *Ethnic Diasporas & Great Power Strategies in Asia*. (Honolulu, Hawaii and New Delhi: India Research Press and the Asia-Pacific Center for Security Studies, 2007.)

Mikhail Alexseev expressed a more cautious approach to Chinese migration of the Russian Far East in his paper "The Chinese are Coming: Public Opinion and Threat Perception in the Russian Far East" (Ponars Policy Memo 184, San Diego State University, January 2001.)

For an excellent history of the Russian conquest of the Far East, see John J. Stephan, *The Russian Far East: A History*, Stanford, California: Stanford University Press, 1994.

Chapter Two

The best overview of the Chinese communities in the Pacific is by Shanghai-born Lynn Pan, (ed.) *The Encyclopedia of the Chinese Overseas* (Singapore: Archipelago Press and the Chinese Heritage Centre, 1998, pp. 292-303). Much background data for this chapter also came from Ron Crocombe's detailed study *Asia in the Pacific Islands: Replacing the West*. Suva (Suva, Fiji: University of the South Pacific, 2007.)

Background information about the Pacific Islands, including Chinese migration, can also be found in Crocombe's other detailed study of the region, *The South Pacific* (Suva, Fiji: University of the South Pacific, 2001.)

In Port Moresby, Steve Marshall of the Australian Broadcasting Corporation, showed me around and helped me with background information.

The quotes from Jerry Singirok and Tarcy Eli come from newspaper clippings in his archives.

Additional information about China's mining ventures in Papua New Guinea comes from Geoffrey York's article "Papua New Guinea and China's New Empire" in *The Globe and Mail*, January 2, 2009. Ben Bohane, an Australian journalist living in Vanuatu, has written extensively about Papua New Guinea's infamous *raskols*, for instance "Rascals: They rape, murder and steal. They're PNG's bandits and they're destroying our nearest neighbour" (*The Bulletin*, June 27, 1995.) Craig Skehan, another Australian journalist specialising in the South Pacific, shared with me internal police documents about passport fraud and illegal migration to Papua New Guinea.

In the Solomon Islands, New Zealand academic Anna Powles guided me around Honiara's Chinatown and shared with me her intimate knowledge of the islands. The report from the Christian Care Centre about logging and child abuse in the Solomons is available online: <http://www.pacifichealthvoices.org/files/Commericial%20Sex%20%20Exp%20in%20Solomon.pdf>

For anyone interested in learning Pidgin English, a good introduction is *Evry samting yu wantem save long Bislama be yu freat tumas blong askem* ("Everything you wanted to know about Bislama but were afraid to ask") by Darrell Tryon

(Singapore: Media Masters, 1997). Bislama is the kind of Pidgin spoken in Vanuatu and the name of Bislama is derived from French word for sea cucumber, "bêche de mer." The first European traders in Vanuatu (then the New Hebrides) came to collect sea cucumbers, and their Creole-type hybrid language they spoke came to be used by the local laborers between themselves, as well as their English- and French-speaking overseers.

Chapter Three

For Polynesia, the best overviews of the various Chinese communities there are also in Lynn Pan's (ed.) *The Encyclopedia of the Chinese Overseas* (Singapore: Archipelago Press and the Chinese Heritage Centre, 1998), and Ron Crocombe's *Asia in the Pacific Islands: Replacing the West.* Suva (Suva, Fiji: University of the South Pacific, 2007.) and *The South Pacific* (Suva, Fiji: University of the South Pacific, 2001.) *The Pacific Islands Yearbook*, published annually by the Fiji Times in Suva, also contains useful data about the region, including its Chinese communities. Bessie Ng Kumlin Ali, whose ancestors came from China's Guangdong province, has documented the history of the Chinese community in Fiji in her *Chinese in Fiji* (Suva: University of the South Pacific, 2002). Chinese migration to Samoa is described in Ben Liuaana (a native Samoan), *Featuna'i's Samoa Tula'i: Ecclesiastical and Political Face of Samoa's Independence, 1900-1962* (Apia, Samoa: Malua Printing Press, 2004.), including excerpts from Nancy W.Y. Tom's 1986 study *The Chinese in Western Samoa, 1875-1985: The Dragon Came From Afar.* The story about the Samoan Nazi comes from Michael Field, *Mau: Samoa's Struggle Against New Zealand Oppression* (Wellington: Reed, 1984, p.217-219. Swedish ethnologist Bengt Danielsson, who accompanied Thor Heyerdahl on the famous Kon-Tiki expedition, has written a book about sexuality in the South Pacific, *Love in the South Seas* (New York: Reynal & Company, 1956.) Shirley Baker's adventures in Tonga are described in Noel Rutherford's *Shirley Baker and the King of Tonga* (Honolulu: University of Hawaii Press, 1996.) A good history of the Indian community in Fiji is Rajendra Prasad's *Tears in Paradise* (Auckland: Glade Publishers, 2004; Prasad is a Fiji-born Indian.) Bessie Ng Kumlin Ali's *Chinese in Fiji* (Suva, Fiji: University of the South Pacific, 2002) is a good history of Fiji's Chinese community. In Suva, the late Robert Keith-Reid, founder and editor of the monthly magazine *Islands Business* showed me around, introduced me to people and shared his extensive knowledge of Fiji and other islands in the Pacific. In Apia, Michael von Reiche, a Samoa-born German, related the history of the Germans in Samoa over beers at the Sails' restaurant on Beach Road. In the Cook Islands, I met Ron Crocombe, the dean of Pacific studies, and local journalists for the *Cook Islands Times* and the *Cook Islands News*. In French Polynesia, I managed to meet the legendary Bengt Danielsson before he passed away in 1997. I also interviewed independence leader Oscar Temaru, then leader of the opposition. I visited the Kuomintang hall in Papeete during a second journey to French Polynesia in March 2008.

Chapter Four

I have outlined more in detail migration and organised crime in Fujian in my book *Bloodbrothers: Crime, Business and Politics in Asia* (Sydney: Allen & Unwin, 2002.) I have also visited both Xiamen in the People's Republic of China, and Jinmen (Quemoy) in the Republic of China. For Chinese migration to Europe, see Pal Nyiri, *New Chinese Migrants in Europe: The Case of the Chinese Community in Hungary* (Aldershot, Brookfield, Singapore and Sydney: Ashgate, 1999.) See also Paul J. Smith (ed.), *Human Smuggling: Chinese Migrant Trafficking and the Challenge to America's Immigration Tradition* (Washington DC: The Centre for Strategic and International Studies, 1997), and David Kyle and Rey Koslowski (eds.) *Global Human Smuggling: Comparative Perspectives* (Baltimore and London: The Johns Hopkins University Press, 2001) as well as Ko-Lin Chin's (Chin Ko-lin's) excellent study *Smuggled Chinese: Clandestine Immigration to the United States* (Philadelphia: Temple University Press, 1999.) The third wave of Chinese migration is also the theme of Pal Nyiri's and Igor Saveliev's (eds.) *Globalising Chinese Migration: Trends in Europe and Asia* (Aldershot: Ashgate Publishing, 2002.) The account of the voyage of the *Golden Venture* comes from my own interviews with former crew members of the ship. An immigration officer at the Department for Homeland Security in Honolulu told me how migrants travel through Narita airport to the United States. He was also the officer who interviewed the asylum seeker mentioned in the text. The case of Peter Swanson in Vanuatu was widely published in a local newspaper, the *Vanuatu Trading Post*, in 2006 and 2007. See also "Digested Reports of the Vanuatu Office of the Ombudsman" <http://www.paclii.org/vu/ombudsmanreports/Vanuatu/Digest/digest_96-01.html>

For a detailed description of the passport scandal in Tonga and the role of the court jester, see Kalafi Moala, *Island Kingdom Strikes Back: The Story of an Independent Island Newspaper — Taimi O Tonga* (Auckland: Pacmedia Publishers, 2002, pp. 113-117; Moala is a prominent Tongan journalist and newspaperman.) In Majuro, the Marshall Islands, I met and interviewed Giff Johnson of the *Marshall Islands Journal* and diplomats from the Embassy of the Republic of China (Taiwan.) The Vanuatu passport affair was related to me by Ombudsman Marie-Noelle Ferrieux Patterson during two visits to Port Vila, Vanuatu. Amarendra Nath Ghosh's visit to Laos was front-page news in the *Vientiane Times* (February 20-22, 2001) under the headline "Laos consolidates relations with Vanuatu." For the strategic implications of Chinese migration to the Pacific, see John Henderson and Benjamin Reilly, "Dragon in Paradise: China's Rising Star in Oceania" (*The National Interest*, Summer 2003) and Susan Windybank, "The China Syndrome" (*Policy*, Vol. 21, No. 2, Winter 2005.)

Chapter Five

I visited Boten in the mid-1990s, when the car smuggling operation was in full swing. For more about Boten today, see *Merchants of Madness: The Methamphetamine Explosion in the Golden Triangle*, pp. 113-115 (Bertil Lintner and Michael Black,

Chiang Mai: Silkworm Books, 2009.) For China's growing influence in Laos, see Denis Gray, "Laos Fears China's Footprint," *Associated Press*, April 6, 2008, and Nga Pham, "China Moves Into Laid-Back Laos," *BBC News*, April 8, 2008. For China's growing influence in Cambodia, see articles with exactly that title by Julio Jeldres in *Africana*, 2002:7-11, and by David Fullbrook in *Asia Times Online*, October 6, 2006. *The Chinese in Cambodia* by William M. Willmott (Vancouver, Canada: University of British Columbia, 1967) is a dated yet comprehensive study of the Chinese community in Cambodia. For an overview of China's and India's respective Burma policies, see Bertil Lintner, "China and South Asia's East," *Himal South Asia Magazine*, October 2002. A good collection of essays about the frontier areas is *Where China Meets Southeast Asia: Social & Cultural Change in the Border Regions* (edited by Grant Evans, Christopher Hutton and Kuah Khun Eng; New York and Singapore: St. Martins Press and the Institute of Southeast Asian Studies, 2000.) For a history of Burma's Indian communities, see Nalini Ranian Chakravarti, *The Indian Minority in Burma: The Rise and Decline of an Immigrant Community* (London: Oxford University Press, 1971.) I have travelled widely in Laos, Cambodia and Yunnan, and live in Chiang Mai in northern Thailand. Over the years, I have met and interviewed numerous sources in all those areas. For a history of China's relations with the CPB, see my book *The Rise and Fall of the Communist Party of Burma* (Ithaca: Cornell University, 1990.) For a good overview of Chinese communities in Southeast Asia, see Martin Smith, *The Chinese of Southeast Asia* (London: Minority Rights Group, 1992.)

Chapter Six

For a good overview of the Triads and overseas Chinese communities, see Lynn Pan, *Sons of the Yellow Emperor: A History of the Chinese Diaspora*. (Boston: Little, Brown and Company, 1990) and my own *Bloodbrothers: Crime, Business and Politics in Asia* (Sydney: Allen & Unwin, 2002.) The quotes from Deng Xiaoping and Wong Man-fong appear in *Bloodbrothers* as well, and were first reported by the Hong Kong daily *South China Morning Post* ("A Social Contract with the Territory's

Underworld," May 14, 1997.) See also *The Triads as Business* (London and New York: Routledge, 2000) by Hong Kong researcher Yiu Kong Chu. Triad initiation rites are described in detail in *Triad Societies in Hong Kong* by W.P. Morgan (Hong Kong: Government Press, 1989.) David Kaplan's *Fires of the Dragon: Politics, Murder, and the Kuomintang* (New York: Atheneum, 1992) deals with the 1984 murder of Henry Liu and the United Bamboo Gang. For the early years of the Triads, see Dian Murray, *The Origins of the Tiandihui: The Chinese Triads in Legend and History* (Stanford, California: Stanford University Press, 1994.) The exploits of "Big-Eared" Du in Shanghai in the 1930s are described in Pan Ling, *Old Shanghai: Gangsters in Paradise* (Singapore: Heinemann Asia, 1993) and Brian G. Martin, *The Shanghai Green Gang: Politics and Organised Crime*, 1919-1937 (Berkeley, California: University of California Press, 1996.) For crime in general in the Pacific, see John Murray, *The Minnows of Triton: Policing, Politics, Crime and Corruption in the South Pacific Islands* (Self-publishing, Australia, 2006.) I met and interviewed police officers in Suva, Fiji, May 2005. In Vanuatu, Ombudsman Marie-Noelle Ferrieux Patterson generously shared information about the banks and fraud in the republic. For an account of events in Burma following the 1989 CPB mutiny, see *Merchants of Madness: The Methamphetamine Explosion in the Golden Triangle* by Bertil Lintner and Michael Black (Chiang Mai: Silkworm Books, 2009) and my own book, *The Rise and Fall of the Communist Party of Burma* (Ithaca: Cornell University, 1990.)

Chapter Seven

Islands Business, a regional monthly published in Fiji, in its February 2004 issue, covered Kiribati's switch to recognition of Taiwan, "Taiwan's Tacky Tactics in Tarawa," which included an interview with the new Kiribati president, Anote Tong. A detailed report on the 2002 election in Kiribati and Taiwan's role in it also appeared in the February 15, 2004 issue of the *Baltimore Sun* ("Taiwan's Pacific Power Play. Kiribati: Struggling for world respect, the 'Republic of China' uses dollar diplomacy, gets recognition from remote Pacific island nation," by Gady A. Epstein.) It was a front-page report in the official *Taiwan Journal*: "Republic of China, Kiribati Forge Ties" (November 14, 2003.) The China-Taiwan rivalry in the Pacific was also analysed by Nicholas Zaminska and Jason Dean, "Islands of Discord in the Pacific" (*The Wall Street Journal*, May 9, 2006.)

Details on the *Yuan Wang* tracking ships can be found at <http://www.globalsecurity.org/military/world/china/yuan-wang.htm>

A good and critical account of the United States' past and present activities in the Marshall Islands is *Collision Course at Kwajalein: Marshall Islanders in the Shadow of the Bomb* (Pacific Resource Centre, Honolulu, 1984) by Giff Johnson. I interviewed not only Johnson, but also James Matayoshi, the mayor of Rongelap Atoll, during my May 2004 visit to the Marshall Island. For Marshall Islands claims for more compensation for the fallout of the nuclear tests, see <http://www.nuclearclaimstribunal.com/>

For the US government's view on security in the Pacific, see *The Southwest Pacific: US Interests and China's Growing Influence* (Washington: Congressional Research Service, July 6, 2007.) The training of Tibetan guerrillas on Saipan island is described in John Kenneth Knaus, *Orphans of the Cold War: America and the Tibetan Struggle for Survival* (New York: Public Affairs, 1999, pp. 140, 146, 148 and 218.) Ben Bohane's article "America's Pacific Build-up" appeared in *The Diplomat*, August 22, 2007. For the first Taiwan-Pacific Allies Summit, see *Taiwan Journal*, September 6, 2006. For Chinese hackers attacking Kevin Rudd's computer and mobile phone, see "Chinese 'Spying' Rattles Australia" by Vivian Wai-yin Kwok, at <http://www.forbes.com/2009/04/03/china-spies-scare-markets-equity-rio.html>

The Canadian "Sidewinder" report is quoted at <http://www.canadafreepress.com/index.php/article/5424>

The complete report is available at <http://www.primetimecrime.com/Articles/RobertRead/Sidewinder%20page%201.htm>

"The Great Game" is a term used for the strategic rivalry between the British Empire and Russia for supremacy in Central Asia in the 19th century. "The New Great Game" is sometimes used to describe the regional rivalry between

India and China; see, for instance, "The New Great Game" by Hannah Beech (*Time* Magazine [Asia], March 19, 2009.)

Chapter Eight

For China's "charm offensive," see Joshua Kurlantzick, *Charm Offensive: How China's Soft Power is Transforming the World* (New Haven and London: Yale University Press/A New Republic Book, 2007.) The United States Congressional Research Service deals with the same issue in *CRS Report for Congress: China's "Soft Power" in Southeast Asia* (Washington: Congressional Research Service, January 4, 2008.) A very informative book on the "new" China is Mette Thunø (ed.), *Beyond Chinatown: New Chinese Migration and the Global Expansion of China* (Copenhagen: Nordic Institute of Asian Studies Press, 2007.) See also Leo Suriyadinata (ed.), *Southeast Asia's Chinese Businesses in an Era of Globalisation* (Singapore: Institute of Southeast Asian Studies, 2006) and Murray Weiderbaum & Samuel Hughes, *The Bamboo Network: How Expatriate Chinese Entrepreneurs are Creating a New Economic Superpower in Asia* (New York: The Free Press, 1996.) More critical views can be found in Michael Backman, *Asian Eclipse: Exposing the Dark Side of Business in Asia* (Singapore, New York: John Wiley & Sons [Asia], 1999) and Alan Dupont, *East Asia Imperilled: Transnational Challenges to Security* (Cambridge, UK: Cambridge University Press, 2001.)

An excellent study of migration in Northeast Asia (including the Russian Far East) is Tsuneo Akaha and Anna Vassilieva (eds.), *Crossing National Borders: Human Migration Issues in Northeast Asia* (Tokyo, New York, Paris: United Nations University Press, 2005.) For a comprehensive history of the Chinese community in Korea, see Shim Jae Hoon's contribution to Lynn Pan's (ed.) *The Encyclopedia of the Chinese Overseas* (Singapore: Archipelago Press and the Chinese Heritage Centre, 1998, pp. 341-343). In the same volume, Syukushin Kyo (Shu-zhen Hsu) writes about the Chinese communities in Japan (pp. 332-339.) Roberty Sutter's paper, "China's Rise in Asia—Promises, Prospects and Implications for the United States," was published by the Asia-Pacific Centre for Security Studies in Honolulu, Hawaii, in February 2005.

BIBLIOGRAPHY

Books and Independent Studies

Akaha, Tsuneo and **Anna Vassilieva** (eds.) *Crossing National Borders: Human Migration Issues in Northeast Asia*. Tokyo, New York and Paris: United Nations University Press, 2005. 254pp. A collection of essays about Chinese migration to the Russian Far East, Chinese, Koreans and Russians in Japan, North Koreans in China, and migration issues in South Korea and Mongolia.

Chin Ko-lin. *Smuggled Chinese: Clandestine Immigration to the United States*. Philadelphia: Temple University Press, 1999. 221pp. An outstanding study of illegal Chinese migration to the United States based on interviews with people who have been smuggled as well as the smugglers themselves.

Choi, C.Y. *Chinese Migration and Settlement in Australia*. Sydney: Sydney University Press, 1975. A study of the history of Chinese settlement in Australia.

Crocombe, Ron. *Asia in the Pacific Islands: Replacing the West*. Suva, Fiji: University of the South Pacific, 2007. 622pp. A detailed study of how China and other Asian countries are replacing the West as the main source of influence in the Pacific.

Dyatlov, Viktor (ed.) *A Bridge Across the Amur River: International Migration and Migrants in Siberia and the Far East*. Moscow and Irkutsk: The Natalis Publishing House, 2004. 430pp. (In Russian and English.) Papers from a workshop on migration to Siberia and the Russian Far East held in Irkutsk in 2004.

Evans, Grant and **Christopher Hutton** and **Kuah Khun Eng** (eds.) *Where China Meets Southeast Asia: Social and Cultural Change in the Border Regions*. New York and Singapore: St. Martin's Press and the Institute of Southeast Asian

Studies, 2000. 346pp. Essays on the meeting of cultures on the border between China and mainland Southeast Asia.

Field, Michael. *Mau: Samoa's Struggle Against New Zealand Oppression.* Wellington: Reed, 1984. 261pp. Contains information about the origin of the Chinese community in Samoa.

Jayasuriya, Leksiri and **Kee Pookong.** *The Asianisation of Australia? Some Facts about the Myths.* Melbourne: Melbourne University Press, 1999. 114pp. An objective account of Asian migration to Australia.

Kurlantzick, Joshua. *Charm Offensive: How China's Soft Power is Transforming the World.* New Haven and London: Yale University Press, 2007. 305pp. A study of the "soft power" of Chinese diplomacy.

Leveau, Arnaud (ed.) *Investigating the Grey Areas of the Chinese Communities in Southeast Asia.* Bangkok: Research Institute of Contemporary Southeast Asia, 2007. 168pp. A collection of papers about Chinese secret societies in Thailand, Chinese communities in Burma, Thailand and Malaysia.

Liuaana, Featuna'i Ben. *Samoa Tula'i: Ecclesiastical and Political Face of Samoa's Independence, 1900-1962.* Apia, Samoa: Malua Printing Press, 2004. 368pp. A history of modern Samoa containing information about early Chinese settlers on the islands.

Murray, John. *The Minnows of Triton: Policing, Politics, Crime and Corruption in the South Pacific Islands.* Self-publishing, Australia, 2006. 299pp. A book about crime in the South Pacific written by an Australian Federal Police officer.

Ng, Bessie Kumlin Ali. *Chinese in Fiji.* Suva, Fiji: University of the South Pacific, 2002. 286pp. A history of the Chinese community in Fiji written by a Fijian-Chinese.

Nyiri, Pal and **Igor Saveliev** (eds.) *Globalizing Chinese Migration.* Aldershot: Ashgate Publishing, 2002. 343pp. Papers from a conference on Chinese migration held in Budapest on May 26-27, 2000.

Pan, Lynn. *Sons of the Yellow Emperor: A History of the Chinese Diaspora.* Boston: Little, Brown and Company, 1990. A best-selling book about Chinese communities overseas.

—. (ed.) *The Encyclopedia of the Chinese Overseas.* Singapore: Archipelago Press and the Chinese Heritage Centre, 1998. 399pp. Contains chapters about Chinese communities all over the world, including the Russian Far East, the South Pacific and Southeast Asia.

Rolls, Eric. *Sojourners: The Epic Story of China's Centuries-old Relationship with Australia.* Brisbane: University of Queensland Press, 1993. 531pp. A comprehensive history of Chinese-Australian relations.

Stephan, John J. *The Russian Far East: A History.* Stanford, California: Stanford University Press, 1994. 481pp. An excellent history of the Russian conquest of the Far East.

Suryadinata, Leo (ed.) *Southeast Asia's Chinese Businesses in the Era of Globalization: Coping With the Rise of China.* Singapore: the Institute of Southeast Asian Studies, 2006. 374pp. This book addresses the rise of China and its impact on Southeast Asia's economies and businesses.

Thuno, Mette (ed.) *Beyond Chinatown: New Chinese Migration and the Global Expansion of China.* Copenhagen: the Nordic Institute of Asian Studies Press, 2007. 281pp. A collection of essays about Chinese migration to various parts of the world.

Travers, Robert. *Australian Mandarin: The Life and Times of Quong Tart.* Kenthurst: Kangaroo Press, 1981. The story of a remarkable Chinese immigrant who became one of the most fascinating characters of colonial Sydney.

Wang Gungwu. *China and the Chinese Overseas.* Singapore: Times Academic Press, 1992. 312pp. A history of Chinese migration which also concentrates on contemporary issues such as the degree of integration with indigenous populations.

Weidenbaum, Murray and **Samuel Hughes**. *The Bamboo Network: How Expatriate Chinese Entrepreneurs are Creating a New Economic Superpower in Asia.* New York: The Free Press, 1996. 264pp. An overview of China's expanding economic influence in Southeast Asia.

Willmott, William. *The Chinese in Cambodia.* Vancouver: University of British Columbia, 1967. 131pp. A history of the old Chinese community in Cambodia.

Wirsing, Robert G. and **Rouben Azizian** (eds.) *Ethnic Diasporas & Great Power Strategies in Asia.* Honolulu, Hawaii and New Delhi: India Research Press and the Asia-Pacific Center for Security Studies, 2007. 355pp. Papers from a conference of migration in the Asia-Pacific region held in Honolulu on October 12-14, 2004.

Articles

Bohane, Ben. "America's Pacific Build-Up." *The Diplomat,* Sept/Oct 2007.

Boucaud, André and **Louis Boucaud.** "Burma: a 24th province of China." *Le Monde Diplomatique,* English edition, November 2006.

Feizkhah, Elizabeth. "Making friends: Beijing is courting the island nations in the Pacific." *Asiaweek,* June 15, 2001.

Davis, Anthony. "Document forgery operations in Thailand." *Jane's Intelligence Review,* February 2005.

Field, Michael. "Power struggle." *The Dominion,* May 31, 2005.

Flicking, David. "Raskol gangs rule the world's city." *Guardian,* September 22, 2004.

Keith-Reid, Robert and **Samisoni Pareti.** "Chopstick Diplomacy: China's Pacific Games." *Islands Business,* March 2006.

Jane's Intelligence Digest. "Chinese organised crime in Russia." Posted February 11, 2009.

Jeldres, Julio. "China's growing influence in Cambodia." *Africana,* 2002:7-11.

Kapetas, Anastasia. "Aimed at China?" *The Diplomat,* Sept/Oct 2007.

Lintner, Bertil. "Bangkok-Taipei-Peking: the unsettling triangle." *Far Eastern Economic Review,* January 24, 1985.

—. "Rocks and a hard place," *Far Eastern Economic Review,* September 9, 1993.

—. "Yunnan-Burma: Enter the Dreams/Cutting Edge/A Piece of the Action." *Far Eastern Economic Review,* December 22, 1994.

—. "World Wide Web." *Far Eastern Economic Review,* May 14, 1998.

—. "The Third Wave." *Far Eastern Economic Review*, June 24, 1999.

—. "Triads tighten grip on Russia's Far East." *Jane's Intelligence Review*, September 2003.

—. "Spreading tentacles/Flying money." *Far Eastern Economic Review*, October 2, 2003.

—. "A new battle for the Pacific." *Far Eastern Economic Review*, August 5, 2004.

—. "The Chinese are coming…to Russia." *Asia Times Online*, May 27, 2006.

—. "Chinese fill void in South Pacific exodus." *Hankyoreh*, November 29, 2006.

—. "America's China Worries: Growing Chinese Presence in the Pacific islands unsettles locals and poses questions for the US." *YaleGlobal Online*, February 13, 2007.

—. "A new breed of immigrants fan out." *Asia Times Online*, April 17, 2007.

—. "The Sinicizing of the South Pacific." *Asia Times Online*, April 18, 2007.

—. "A how-to guide for fleeing China." *Asia Times Online*, April 19, 2007.

Reilly, Benjamin and **John Henderson**. "Dragon in Paradise: China's Rising Star in Oceania." *The National Interest*, No. 72, Summer 2003.

Seneviratne, Kalinga. "South Pacific: Fear of domination sparked anti-Chinese riots." *Inter Press Service*, April 22, 2006.

Shambaugh, David. "China engages Asia: Reshaping the Regional Order." *International Security*, Vol. 29, No 3 (Winter 2004).

Shie, Tamara Renee. "China woos the South Pacific." *Asia Times Online*, March 29, 2006.

Sutter, Robert. "China's rise in Asia: Promises, prospects and implications for the United States." *Asia-Pacific Center for Security Studies*. February 2005.

Wheeler, Matthew. "China expands its southern sphere of influence." *Jane's Intelligence Review*, June 2005.

Windybank, Susan. "The China syndrome." *Policy*, Vol. 21, No 2. Winter 2005.

Yin Soeum. "Cambodia feels China's hard edge." *Asia Times Online*, December 8, 2006.

York, Geoffrey. "Papua New Guinea and China's New Empire." *The Globe and Mail*, January 2, 2009.

Zamiska, Nicholas and **Jason Dean.** "Islands of discord in the Pacific." *The Wall Street Journal*, May 9, 2006.

INDEX

ABOUT THE AUTHOR

BERTIL LINTNER was born in 1953 in Sweden of mixed Swedish-Austrian parentage. In his teens, he hitch-hiked around Europe and spent some time in West Africa. He came to Asia in 1975 on the overland route from Europe to Australia. Bertil spent five years on the road in Asia, from Istanbul to Bangkok and from Denpasar to Tokyo, before settling down in Thailand in 1980. His early travels were financed by the income from odd jobs in Sweden, New Zealand, Hong Kong and Japan.

In 1980 he decided to become a free-lance writer and soon established himself as an authority on insurgency in Burma. He now contributes to a number of publications in Asia and Europe and contributed regularly to the *Far Eastern Economic Review* in Hong Kong, until its demise in December, 2009. His other books include:

Land of Jade (3rd, revised edition published by Orchid Press; Bangkok, 2011)

Outrage: Burma's Struggle for Democracy

The Rise and Fall of the Communist Party of Burma

Burma in Revolt: Opium and Insurgency Since 1948

Bloodbrothers: Crime, Business and Politics in Asia

Great Leader, Dear Leader: Demystifying North Korea Under the Kim Clan

Lightning Source UK Ltd.
Milton Keynes UK
UKOW051412030912

198406UK00001B/10/P